Strategi Management Control

– with a focus on dialogue

FREDRIK NILSSON

CARL-JOHAN PETRI

ALF WESTELIUS

(EDS.)

Translation: Marcia Halvorsen

Studentlitteratur

Original title: *Strategisk ekonomistyrning – med dialog i fokus*
© Studentlitteratur 2016

Art. No 39331
ISBN 978-91-44-11442-2
First edition
1:1

© The authors and Studentlitteratur 2016
studentlitteratur.se
Studentlitteratur AB, Lund

Translation: Marcia Halvorsen
Cover design: Jens Martin/Signalera
Cover illustration: Pressmaster/Shutterstock.com

Printed by GraphyCems, Spain 2016

CONTENTS

FOREWORD

It is with great pleasure we present this book on strategic management control. Our purpose is to offer insights regarding the area of strategic management control, with particular reference to the developmental work of Professor Nils-Göran Olve.

Fifteen authors contributed to the book. In addition to the three editors, the other authors are the following: Professor Christian Ax; Professor Bino Catasús; Associate Professor Mikael Cäker; Assistant Professor Mathias Cöster; fmr Professor Thomas Falk; Assistant Professor Cecilia Gullberg; Associate Professor Einar Iveroth; Assistant Professor Erik Jannesson; Professor Johnny Lind; Associate Professor Jan Lindvall; Jan Roy; and Associate Professor Åke Walldius. Together, these authors describe strategic management control. Most of the authors are active primarily in academia as teachers, supervisors and researchers. All of us are very interested in how management control is exercised – so that we can learn more about the area from contemporary organisations and companies and develop new theories and concepts that can be of practical use.

Because of our experience as researchers and teachers at various Swedish universities, we are convinced our book is of national, educational interest in Sweden. The book deals with issues and theories related to strategic management control that are appropriate at the C Level (Bachelor) and at the D Level (Master) in Swedish higher education. We also think our approach – a Scandinavian approach to strategic management control – makes the book internationally relevant.

We thank all the authors for their contributions, as well as their very productive cooperation throughout the entire book project. The breadth of knowledge, the diversity of research traditions and the authors' insights into the design, use and effect of strategic management control impressed us – time and time again. Owing to their contributions, we think the book explains how strategic management control is exercised successfully (or not). We also thank our publisher Eric Rehn, our editor Carina Blohmé, the translator Marcia Halvorsen and the proofreader Marion Söderström for their constructive efforts throughout the project.

Uppsala, Brussels and Saltsjöbaden: September 2016

Fredrik Nilsson, Carl-Johan Petri and *Alf Westelius*

NOTES ON THE CONTRIBUTORS

Christian Ax is Professor of Business Administration, specialising in Management Accounting, at the School of Business, Economics and Law at the University of Gothenburg. He is currently researching the diffusion of management accounting innovations, the design and use of management control systems as a package, and the relation between dimensions of competition and the design of customer accounting systems.

Bino Catasús is Professor of Business Administration, specialising in Accounting and Auditing, in the Department of Business Studies at Stockholm University. In his current research he focuses on how numbers influence and are influenced by society. He has published a number of books and scientific articles on both financial accounting and management control.

Mikael Cäker is Associate Professor of Business Administration, specialising in Management Control, at the School of Business, Economics and Law at the University of Gothenburg. In his current research he focuses on inter-organisational controls, reward systems and the interaction among various control elements. He also researches the ability of organisations to manage the external pressures to increase control.

Mathias Cöster holds a PhD and is Assistant Professor in the Department of Business Studies at Uppsala University Campus Gotland. He has a Doctorate in Economic Information Systems from Linköping University. Since 2009 he has been active in the research network CASIP (the Centre for Advanced Studies in Innovative Price Models), a research collaboration project between academia and industry that studies strategic perspectives on pricing and the development of price models. The work of CASIP has resulted in the publication of a book and several articles. He teaches and manages courses in accounting at Uppsala University, Campus Gotland.

Thomas Falk has been Professor in the Department of Management and Engineering/Industrial Economics at Linköping University. In his research he has focused on the influence of information technology on the economy and on society.

Cecilia Gullberg has a Doctorate in Business Administration and is a researcher in the Department of Business Studies at Uppsala University. She is also a lecturer in Business Studies at Södertörn University. In her current research she focuses on the interface between management accounting and management, and on managers' use of accounting information in relation to other types of information.

Einar Iveroth is Associate Professor in the Department of Business Studies at Uppsala University. In his current research he focuses on strategic pricing and price models, organisational change and control, and technological change. He has published his work in a wide variety of international scholarly journals and his most recent book is *Effective Organizational Change: Leading through Sensemaking* (Routledge, 2016).

Erik Jannesson is Assistant Professor in the Department of Management and Engineering at Linköping University as well as a partner of the consulting firm Serus that advises on project and business development. The focus of his research, teaching and consultancy work is strategic management control from social, environmental and financial perspectives. In his most recent research project he studied the organisation and management control of social investments.

Johnny Lind is Professor and Head of the Department of Accounting at the Stockholm School of Economics, and a part-time full professor (Professor II) at the Trondheim Business School. In his current research he focuses on the effects of managerial control on inter-organisational relationships and the influence of capital markets on companies' control and operations. His latest two books are *Innovation eller kvartalskapitalism* (2013, Liber) and *Morgondagens industri* (2011, Studentlitteratur).

Jan Lindvall is Associate Professor in the Department of Business Studies at Uppsala University. He researches and teaches in the area of performance management, with a special interest in how access to IT solutions such as ERP, business intelligence and "cloud" solutions influence operational organisation and management. He is also a lecturer and consultant in the area of knowledge management.

Fredrik Nilsson has been Professor of Business Studies, specialising in Accounting, at Uppsala University since 2010. Previously he was Professor of Economic Information Systems at Linköping University. In his research he focuses on how different information systems (e.g. related to financial accounting, management control and production control) are designed and used in formulating and implementing strategies.

Carl-Johan Petri is Assistant Professor of Economic Information Systems at Linköping University. He has worked with management control development for more than 20 years. He is mainly interested in the use of strategy maps and balanced scorecards, both in research and practice. He has published several books on the balanced scorecard that have been translated into a dozen languages.

Jan Roy is the Chairman of the Board of several companies, including Kairos Future (an international consulting/research company). He is also a member of the research advisory board at Mid Sweden University's research group, Etour, which focuses on tourism. He was previously the CEO for Parks and Resorts Scandinavia, as well as a manager of a consulting firm that focused on research related to corporate issues. He has contributed to a number of books on the balanced scorecard.

Åke Walldius is Associate Professor of Human Computer Interaction at the Royal Institute of Technology (KTH) in Stockholm. Because of his background in media studies and 15 years of experience as a consultant in Information Visualisation, he is especially interested in how narratives and visualisation technology interact in successful IT and media projects. Using the methodology from genre and design pattern analysis, he researches how successful solutions can be reused, varied and renewed.

Alf Westelius is Professor at Linköping University, specialising in how new and mature organisations navigate and function in the ever-more digitised and dynamic world. People build, manage/control and shape organisations. Therefore, a corner-stone of his research and consulting is Perspectives Management, identifying and paying heed to perspective differences among people. His analyses pay attention both to the specific and the general, and often transcend borders between the private, public and not-for-profit sectors.

1. Strategic management control in theory and practice

FREDRIK NILSSON, CARL-JOHAN PETRI
& ALF WESTELIUS

Strategic management control, which we focus on in this book, differs from traditional management control in several important respects. First, strategic management control supports both strategy formulation and strategy implementation. Second, strategic management control is to a large extent based on non-financial information. Third, strategic management control supports not only tactical decision-making but also strategic and operational decision-making and acting. Fourth, and perhaps most important, strategic management control is designed for, and adapted to, the organisation's unique strategies.

In practice, however, it can be difficult to differentiate between strategic management control and traditional management control. Of course, some organisations may implement a strategic management control system consistent with the idealised version presented in textbooks. Yet most organisations apply both strategic and more traditional management tools in their control systems.

For at least 50 years, the concept of management control has been linked to strategy (see for example Anthony, 1965). One important researcher in the field of strategic management control is Nils-Göran Olve, a Swedish professor whose work in the field is well known in Sweden and elsewhere. Already in his doctoral dissertation, in the 1970s, Olve focused on multiobjective control.[1] It was therefore a natural step for him, in the mid-1990s, to write the first Swedish book about the balanced scorecard: *Balanced Scorecard i Svensk praktik* [translated into English: *Performance Drivers: A Practical Guide to Using the Balanced Scorecard*] (Olve et al., 1997, 1999). That book was translated into more than ten languages and was very successful both in Sweden and abroad.

In the following years Olve participated extensively in discussions on the balanced scorecard, for example as a conference speaker and as author of popular and scientific articles. He co-authored several books on the balanced scorecard, both in English and Swedish (e.g. Olve & Sjöstrand, 2002; Olve et al., 2003; Petri & Olve, 2014a, 2014b). He also wrote about strategic management control in various other publications such as *Controllerhandboken* [in English: *The Controller Handbook*] (Nilsson & Olve, 2013) and *Controlling for Competitiveness: Strategy Formulation and Implementation through Management Control* (Nilsson et al., 2011). Olve's interest in strategic management control, in particular how such control can be exercised, is also reflected in his other areas of interest: network-based organisations (see for example Hedberg et al., 1997), IT's strategic importance (see for example Falk & Olve, 1996), and the controller's various roles (see for example Olve, 2013).

Long before some of these topics of management control

---

1 Multiobjective control deals with the development of control in organisations in which there is more than one main goal. For example, an organisation may simultaneously seek to be a responsible employer, to achieve high financial returns, to serve economically disadvantaged regions, and to reduce its environmental footprint.

became fashionable in research circles in the late 1900s and the early 2000s, Olve had already shown an interest in them. In his 1977 dissertation (*Multiobjective Budgetary Planning: Models for Interactive Planning in Decentralized Organizations*), Olve focused on, among other things, the premise behind the concept of balanced control, namely that an organisation has many different objectives. Specifically, he addressed the budgeting process: it needs to encompass aspects crucial to the organisation's long-term survival, not just financial aspects. He also drew attention to the importance of dialogues (note the term "interactive planning" in the title of his dissertation) in the planning process in decentralised organisations.

Olve has also been interested in the balance between rational and intuitive decision-making. In his 1985 book *Beslutsfattande: en tänkebok om rationella och intuitiva beslut* [in English: *Decision-making: A Protocol for Rational and Intuitive Decision-making*], Olve took a broader perspective on how people make decisions, similar to Kahneman's reasoning in *Thinking, Fast and Slow* (2011). Olve's ideas on the various fundamental mental processes involved in decision-making laid the groundwork for his work on theories and models related to strategic management control.

Nils-Göran Olve has thus had a major influence on the development of knowledge and practice in the field of strategic management control. In this anthology we, the fifteen authors, have collaborated in exploring what we find to be central to and characteristic of a modern Scandinavian approach to the field. In addition to painting this image of issues important to the future of management control (from both theoretical and practical perspectives), we pay tribute to Olve's extensive body of work in this field. The book reviews developments in strategic management control, and looks forward to further developments. In our endeavour, recurrent themes in Olve's books, articles, and chapters, and in his activities as supervisor, instructor, and lecturer, have inspired us – the editors and the chapter authors.

Our ambition in anthologising these contributions into a comprehensive picture of the current state of the field and its central developing trends is to produce a useful book for students, practitioners and scholars. The book, which emphasises the challenges involved in achieving successful strategic management control, aims to present a critical analysis rather than a "simplified solution to problems that are difficult to solve". Clearly, we do not subscribe to the view that the practice of strategic management control consists of more or less meaningless rituals, with only ceremonial implications. On the contrary, our ambition is to emphasise the opportunities afforded by strategic management control, while still recognising its difficulties and challenges.

The book is loosely structured around the planning and follow-up processes (in that order) in strategic management control.

Chapter 2 by Thomas Falk, Carl-Johan Petri, Jan Roy and Åke Walldius is titled "Illustrating an organisation's strategy as a map". The authors describe how the strategy map – a development of the balanced scorecard – can be used to facilitate communication and dialogue on organisational strategy. In part, the chapter is based on the traditional interpretation of what a strategy map is (according to Kaplan and Norton) and in part on other experiences that give the readers additional insights. First, using references to cinema studies, the chapter deepens our understanding of picture-based narratives. Second, the chapter presents a comprehensive description, using a strategy map, of the consequences of digitalisation for companies and organisations. Third, the chapter presents an empirical overview of how the Swedish amusement group – Parks and Resorts Scandinavia (that owns Gröna Lund's Tivoli, Kolmården Wildlife Park, Skara Sommarland, Furuviksparken and Aquaria) – uses strategy maps to facilitate dialogue about the group's strategic direction and ensures that the key performance indicators in the management control system are based in the strategy.

Chapter 3 by Alf Westelius and Johnny Lind is titled "Painting the relevant organisation". The authors discuss how it is increasingly less self-evident which entity should be the focus of strategic management control. Although the relevant organisation may be the whole, or some parts, of an organisation, it may also be a somewhat broader entity such as a joint venture, an imaginary (i.e. virtual) organisation, a network, a value constellation or a partnership. The chapter discusses all these, less obvious, possibilities. Because different people are likely to have different views on what constitutes the relevant entity, an essential aspect of strategic management control is establishing and maintaining the dialogue on associations and boundaries. The dialogue may involve a strong party, perhaps aiming to inspect and influence external parties (e.g. suppliers and customers), but can also be conducted among more equal partners. The authors conclude that people who want to take an active management role, or who want to include others in the exercise of management control, should learn how to paint a convincing picture of what they view as the relevant entity to control (or the relevant parties that should cooperate in jointly controlling their collaboration).

Chapter 4 by Erik Jannesson and Fredrik Nilsson is titled "Planning for control and evaluation". The authors address organisational control and evaluation – the fundamental elements of strategic management control. The literature often discusses the difficulties associated with exercising control and making evaluations. One difficulty is achieving a consensus on which *metrics* to use, which *decisions* are needed to achieve the desired results, and how *responsibility* should be allocated. The authors emphasise that consensus on these matters can be achieved by talking about intended and realised strategies, possible future strategies and the development of business activities. The organisation's various control tools and the relationships among them provide the framework (i.e. the control package or the control mix) for such dialogues. Moreover, the authors address the advantages of coherent planning and evaluation – known as integrated control – and how new IT solutions create possibilities for achieving integrated control.

Chapter 5 by Christian Ax, Mathias Cöster, and Einar Iveroth is titled "Strategic pricing: The relationship between strategy, price models, and product cost". Although pricing is an area of strategic importance, the academic business literature has not addressed the topic to any great extent. In their examination of the linkage between business models, price models and cost models, the authors emphasise that the organisation's business strategy should be the starting point for the development of its pricing strategy and its choice of a relevant cost model. They state that the second starting point is the business model – how the organisation plans to convert its strategy to value for its customers, co-workers[2], and owners. The translation of the goals in the business strategy to specific prices based on accurate calculations of the cost of the product is a difficult task that requires a structure – a price model – to support the work. The chapter presents a meta-model for analysing and understanding the characteristics of various price models: the price model equaliser. One aim of this meta-model is to describe and compare various price models in order to ensure that they are consistent with the organisation's strategies. Choices regarding the business model and the price model must also be consistent with these strategies. Therefore, it is also important to choose a costing model that takes explicit account of the customers' willingness to pay. As a complement to the price model equaliser, the chapter presents a customer-oriented costing model: the Value Creation Model (VCM).

Chapter 6 by Bino Catasús and Mikael Cäker is titled "Controlling and being controlled". The authors are interested in the dialogue about control, and address the challenges of encouraging middle managers and co-workers to agree on and work together towards local goals that are simultaneously acceptable to them and to senior executives. One trend that can hamper the dialogue between various decision-makers in an organisation is that control has become very extensive and complex. Many organisations are overloaded by control processes. Some researchers even describe this as an overdose of control. In such situations, control with many different goals can result in confusion and loss of focus. While ideas

---

2 "Co-worker" is the term used in this book for people who have non-managerial positions. We recognise that some of the cited authors use the word "employee".

about control packages and integrated control may be easy to formulate, it is much more difficult to achieve their intended results in practice. Although today we have the technical resources to manage large amounts of data, those resources do not necessarily direct the way forward. The authors argue that useful dialogues require a common understanding of what the numbers mean and propose that the greatest challenge is to create a dialogue on goals and strategies that reflects the diversity of opinions and ideas in the organisation.

Chapter 7 by Cecilia Gullberg and Jan Lindvall is titled "The controller's role". The authors identify the controller as a key actor in creating strategic management control. Specifically, they focus on the controller's role with particular reference to organisational monitoring and evaluation meetings. They focus on this aspect because of insufficient emphasis in the literature on monitoring and evaluation of achievement of plans and goals. The authors also claim that insights from the area of decision theory lead to changes in the controller's role. Nils-Göran Olve's popular model of the controller's four roles (accountant, educator, analyst and coach) also motivates the chapter. According to the authors, in today's complex organisations it is not enough to exercise control based solely on numerical data. For example, the controller, as educator and coach, needs to understand how to manage social and group-dynamic processes. It is necessary to strike a balance between "sense and sensibility" – that is, between reason and emotion. Although historically, the controller has had a powerful position as the defender of logic, it has become increasingly important to help managers and co-workers find motivation and meaning in their daily work. Therefore, the controller must take an interest in how emotions and values influence people's behaviour and, ultimately, the entire business activity.

In Chapter 8, Conclusions, the editors summarise the book's chapters and highlight some of their important themes and ideas.

As mentioned above, the book is loosely structured according to the logic of an organisation's planning and follow-up processes – from the development and visualisation of the organisation's strategies to the controller's work in monitoring if intended actions have been taken and the goals have been reached. Chapters 2 to 7 present the links in this chain of words to action. They also emphasise the importance of dialogue in strategic management control. Indeed, this feature may be a distinguishing feature of a Scandinavian approach to management.[3] The authors do not think co-workers and partners will agree, submissively, to decisions taken only at the top of the organisational hierarchy. Instead, the authors repeatedly emphasise the importance of dialogue between the various hierarchical levels and among the actors in the network. Nils-Göran Olve's ideas on good management control have probably influenced the authors in their conclusion that dialogue and interaction are the most important success factors in creating a strategic management control system.

We now turn to these six chapters. In the next chapter, we learn more about the characteristics of strategic management control in a narrative that explains how strategies can be documented and described in a way that lays the groundwork for

---

3 For a completely different view of leadership and management, we recommend Jeffrey Pfeffer's book *Leadership BS* (2015).

dialogue and that ensures that the performance indicators in the planning and follow-up processes are strategically relevant.

References

Anthony, Robert N. (1965). *Planning and Control Systems: A Framework for Analysis.* Boston: Harvard University Graduate School of Business Administration.

Falk, Thomas & Olve, Nils-Göran (1996). *IT som strategisk resurs: företagsekonomiska perspektiv och ledningens ansvar.* Stockholm: Liber.

Hedberg, Bo, Dahlgren, Göran, Hansson, Jörgen & Olve, Nils-Göran (1997). *Virtual Organizations and Beyond: Discover Imaginary Systems.* Chichester: John Wiley & Sons.

Kahneman, Daniel (2011). *Thinking, Fast and Slow.* New York: Farrar, Strauss and Giroux.

Nilsson, Fredrik & Olve, Nils-Göran (Eds.) (2013). *Controllerhandboken.* Stockholm: Liber.

Nilsson, Fredrik, Olve, Nils-Göran & Parment, Anders (2011). *Controlling for Competitiveness: Strategy Formulation and Implementation through Management Control.* Malmö and Copenhagen: Liber and Copenhagen Business School Press.

Olve, Nils-Göran (1977). *Multiobjective Budgetary Planning: Models for Interactive Planning in Decentralized Organizations.* Stockholm: EFI.

Olve, Nils-Göran (1985). *Beslutsfattande: en tänkebok om rationella och intuitiva beslut.* Malmö: Liber.

Olve, Nils-Göran (2013). Controlleruppdraget, in Nilsson, Fredrik & Olve, Nils-Göran (Eds.) *Controllerhandboken.* Stockholm: Liber, pp. 78–90.

Olve, Nils-Göran, Petri, Carl-Johan, Roy, Jan & Roy, Sofie (2003). *Framgångsrikt styrkortsarbete – metoder och erfarenheter.* Malmö: Liber.

Olve, Nils-Göran, Roy, Jan & Wetter, Magnus (1997). *Balanced Scorecard i svensk praktik: ledningsverktyg för strategisk verksamhetsstyrning.* Malmö: Liber.

Olve, Nils-Göran, Roy, Jan & Wetter, Magnus (1999). *Performance Drivers: A Practical Guide to Using the Balanced Scorecard.* Chichester: John Wiley & Sons.

Olve, Nils-Göran & Sjöstrand, Anna (2002). *The Balanced Scorecard.* Oxford: Capstone Publishing.

Petri, Carl-Johan & Olve, Nils-Göran (2014a). *Balanserad styrning: utveckling och tillämpning i svensk praktik.* Stockholm: Liber.

Petri, Carl-Johan & Olve, Nils-Göran (2014b). *Strategibaserad styrning: så använder du strategikartor och styrkort för att nå organisationens mål.* Stockholm: Liber.

Pfeffer, Jeffrey (2015). *Leadership BS: Fixing Workplaces and Careers – One Truth at a Time.* New York: Harper Business.

2. Illustrating an organisation's strategy as a map

THOMAS FALK, CARL-JOHAN PETRI, JAN ROY
& ÅKE WALLDIUS

In this chapter we show how a graphic illustration (the strategy map) can facilitate communication and dialogue on an organisation's strategy (between managers and co-workers) and ensure that the key performance indicators (KPIs) in the on-going management control processes are relevant measures of the realisation of the chosen strategy. Our starting point in this discussion is the assumption that an organisation knows how it wants to conduct its activities to achieve its goals, i.e. it has a strategy.[1] In this context it is irrelevant whether the goal is, for example, to generate returns to the shareholders or to fulfil an important mission in society. Regardless of the organisation's goal(s), it is essential that managers and co-workers agree on how they should work to reach them.

The literature on business strategy has focused more on the content of the strategies than on how they can be described and communicated so that everyone in the organisation understands and internalises them. This chapter deals with how the

---

1 Of course, an organisation's strategy is not fixed. Rather, the strategy should take into account new findings on which actions seem to work and which to discard. The balanced scorecard can assist the co-workers in the organisation to see if the strategy takes the organisation closer to its goals or if it is time to change strategy.

chosen strategy can be described to facilitate communication and direct the organisation in the desired direction.

In the chapter, we elaborate on how a specific model, the strategy map, which was developed in the field of management control, can be used to describe an organisation's strategy. In the early 1990s, the researchers and consultants Robert Kaplan and David Norton suggested a performance measurement model to make the management control more long-term and multidimensional. They named their model the Balanced Scorecard. Over time, this model has developed in the direction of strategy execution so the focus is – to a large extent – on the actual execution of the strategy. In the late 1990s, Kaplan and Norton suggested a format for describing the content of a strategy and for translating that content to relevant key performance indicators in the balanced scorecard. They called this format the strategy map.

This chapter consists of four parts. We begin with a short introduction to strategy maps and balanced scorecards. We then broaden our view on strategy maps with a brief reference to cinema studies. We think the field of storytelling has a lot to offer in improving the way we tell the story of the strategy. Next we explain how to address Information Technology (IT) and its effects in a strategy map. We conclude the chapter with an example of how Parks and Resorts Scandinavia (hereafter, PRS), an amusement park group, has used strategy maps to communicate its strategy and to make the management control more strategy-based.

2.1 A brief look back – Where do strategy maps come from?

In the mid-1980s, Robert Kaplan, with Thomas Johnson, criticised traditional management control (Johnson & Kaplan, 1987). Among other things, they criticised companies' one-sided financial focus in their management control systems. Not satisfied with merely pointing to the problem, Kaplan, working with, among others, David Norton, offered a number of solutions to the problems addressed in the book *Relevance Lost*.

Kaplan and Norton suggested that the problem with a too one-sided financial focus in the planning and monitoring processes could be solved, for example with a more balanced performance report. In such a report – in a balanced scorecard – the organisation would be able to see both if it had reached its financial goals, and if it had executed all necessary actions to remain successful today and tomorrow (Kaplan & Norton, 1992). Also, the balanced scorecard should show both the organisation's internal results and external results, from the following four perspectives[2]: financial perspective, customer perspective, internal business process perspective, and the learning and growth perspective (i.e. development) (see Figure 2.1). The result is a balanced control system, both in time (yesterday–today–tomorrow) and in space (internal–external).

---

2 Kaplan and Norton's original text clearly defined which perspectives a balanced scorecard should have. The terms used for their perspectives have varied. We avoid describing these variations and mainly use the four terms noted above. Sometimes, however, when we refer to other authors who have used different terms, we use their terms. We will not discuss the pros and cons of the various terms that have been used.

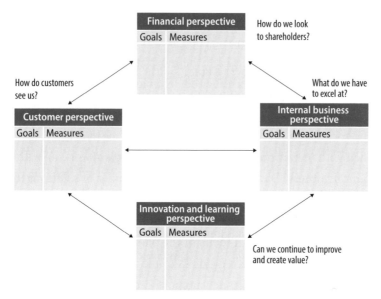

Figure 2.1 Representation of Kaplan and Norton's first visualisation of the linkages among the perspectives in the balanced scorecard (1992, p. 72). The perspectives influence each other bidirectionally.

The concept of the balanced scorecard had an immediate and significant effect.[3] Soon after their first article was published in the *Harvard Business Review* in 1992, Kaplan and Norton published two more articles (1993, 1996a) followed by a still more comprehensive book. It both elaborated on the conceptual framework and presented various examples of different organisations' use of the balanced scorecard (1996b).

---

3 In their yearly survey of the use of management concepts, the global management consulting firm, Bain & Company, found that 40% to 60% of the respondents said they typically use "balanced scorecard" and are satisfied with them. Since 1996 the satisfaction rating has been around four points on a five-point scale [www.bain.com/publications/articles/management-tools-balanced-scorecard.aspx].

Business strategies were a latent idea in Kaplan and Norton's early work on the balanced scorecard. Yet the key performance indicators, as such, received the most attention based on the assumption that they influence behaviour. According to the management cliché, "what you measure is what you get" (Kaplan & Norton, 1992, p. 71).

Many organisations tested the balanced scorecard during the late twentieth century. Their experiences were mixed. Companies that were satisfied with their use of the balanced scorecard often participated in conferences where they explained how their management processes had improved so they managed to execute their strategies and achieve their goals to a greater extent (Ax & Bjørnenak, 2005; Käll, 2005). Word of the balanced scorecard's advantages spread in the Scandinavian countries. However, critics claimed that the balanced scorecard was merely an additional administrative burden – an exercise in number crunching with no positive results (Nørreklit, 2000, 2003).

The too narrow focus on key performance indicators inspired Kaplan and Norton to propose that the balanced scorecard should be supplemented with an additional description to show how the indicators linked to the strategy. Kaplan and Norton (in their early work) and Olve et al. (1997) offered theoretical support for this proposal, and also gave some examples of how the indicators could be linked to strategy. But it was not until the late 1990s that Kaplan and Norton offered an explicit method to directly link the strategy with the indicators in the balanced scorecard. In the beginning, they did not even give their method a name. Instead they wrote about it in general terms; about the need to show the inter-relationships between the four perspectives. Previously they had treated these as bidirectional (see Figure 2.1). Their new, more strategy-based, visualisation illustrates the relationships as unidirectional: from learning and growth to internal business processes, from internal business processes to customers, and from customers to finance (Kaplan & Norton, 1996a, p. 83; see Figure 2.2).

Companies usually document their strategies in specific strategy statements in their business plans. Because such statements are typically for internal use only, it is difficult for external parties to examine them. Hence, to illustrate what such documents may look like, we refer to an example from a public institution that we are very familiar with: Linköping University, Sweden. Linköping University describes its strategy in seven written documents[4] that total more than 100 closely written pages.[5]

When Kaplan and Norton presented their idea about a strategy map, their ambition was to introduce a format that would facilitate the description and communication of what is most important in the strategy, as well as to facilitate translation of it to relevant performance indicators in the management control system.

The strategy map is a graphic illustration, often supplemented by short explanatory texts related to the central

---

4 The strategy is described, among other places, in *Forsknings- och utbild-ningsstrategi*, in *Strategi för internationalisering vid Linköpings universitet*, and in *Strategisk plan för informationsförsörjningen vid Linköpings universitet* [https://www.liu.se/om-liu/strategi/policies?l=sv; 2015-06-05].
5 Linköping University also summarises its strategy as a map, albeit a map that is slightly different from the map that Kaplan and Norton propose [www.liu.se/insidan/strategier/startsida-3/1.519961/LiU_strategikarta_2013-eng.pdf, 2015-06-05].

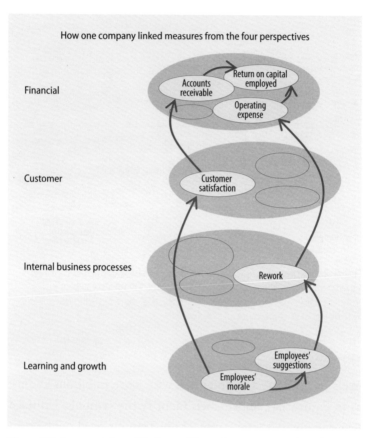

How one company linked measures from the four perspectives

Financial

Customer

Internal business processes

Learning and growth

Figure 2.2 Representation of Kaplan and Norton's more strategy-based visualisation of the linkages between the perspectives in the balanced scorecard (1996a, p. 83). The perspectives influence each other unidirectionally.

concepts in the strategy. Areas and activities that the organisation must work with in order to achieve its goals are structured and described according to the four perspectives of the balanced scorecard. The strategy map usually presents these areas and activities as graphic symbols (sometimes as simple

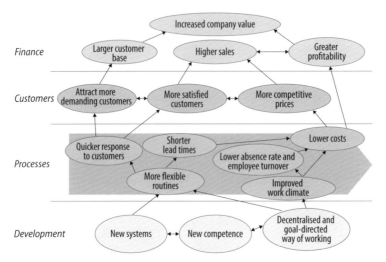

Figure 2.3 An example of the traditional design of a strategy map. The map shows how the packaging company Smurfit Kappa wants to use IT to increase its company value (based on Ivarsen et al,. 2011a, p. 8, our translation from Swedish to English).

ovals, as in Figure 2.3; sometimes with more ambitious idioms, as in Figure 2.4). Short labels identify the symbols. Unlike a text document, these graphical illustrations need not be read linearly in a particular direction. It is just as easy to read the map from top to bottom as bottom to top. The narrative may begin with the financial goals, continuing with a description of the path to those goals (top to bottom). Or the narrative may begin with the organisation's development activities that will impact the internal business processes that will create value for customers, which in turn is expected to lead to positive financial results in the long term (bottom to top).

Figure 2.4 An example of a strategy map designed with a focus on graphic illustrations. The map does not label the perspectives. However, the map is consistent with the balanced scorecard's logic: financial, customer, internal business processes, and learning and growth. See Section 2.5 for a more detailed description of how Parks and Resorts Scandinavia (owners of Gröna Lund's Tivoli, Kolmården Wildlife Park and Skara Sommarland) use their strategy maps. We have kept the Swedish labels in the map since it is the graphical format that is of interest in this figure.

2.2 Features of the Swedish interpretation of strategy maps

Nils-Göran Olve is one of the most prolific Swedish writers on the subjects of strategy maps and balanced scorecards. In his first book (in Swedish) on the balanced scorecard, Olve et al. (1997) devoted some attention to strategy maps. Strategy maps were also an important feature in other publications such as the book by Olve et al. (2003) and the UsersAwards research by Ivarsen et al. (2011b) on usable IT. Petri and Olve (2014a, b) also described

Gröna Lund's work with strategy maps, by explaining the company's use of strategy maps to clarify strategy and by facilitating dialogue among the many co-workers in the organisation.

In Olve's view, there are primarily two recurrent points that differentiate his interpretation from Kaplan and Norton's proposition. First, the characteristics of the process of developing relevant content in the strategy map. Second, the perception of the relationships in the strategy map.

Olve et al. (2003) often return to the idea that the process of developing a strategy map is not merely a simple transcription of existing strategy documents (or ideas about the strategy). Instead, the design of the strategy map should strive to capture an emotion, where as much emphasis should be given to the choice of words and descriptions as to the content. Olve compares the work of documenting a strategy in a strategy map to the work of translating a poem:

> It is somewhat similar to translating a poem from a remote language like Chinese. To understand the meaning of the poem you need a good understanding of Chinese. But this is usually not enough for rewriting it into an English poem. This requires the assistance of a poet who is highly skilled in English. He may not understand much of Chinese but should be skilled at creating a memorable English text. In a similar way, managers discussing their strategic logic may not be able to express it in the most communicative way. The process of formulating scorecards or strategy maps often benefits from having an experienced scorecard process leader – an in-house expert or an outside consultant. But managers must be able themselves to arrive at a good strategy – no consultant can provide this for them.
>
> OLVE ET AL., 2003, P. 147

This work makes great demands on the creator – more than Kaplan and Norton suggest. For example, the usability of generic elements in the strategy map (see the discussion on strategic themes below) is, as Kaplan and Norton suggest, rather small. Describing the strategy in the map instead begins with a blank piece of paper (albeit with the four perspectives as a foundation). This requires a certain artistic touch by the creators as they try to capture the essence of the organisation's strategy in a suggestive and interesting way (see more about the process of creating commitment and participation in describing the strategy later in this chapter, when we take inspiration from how cinema studies understand narratives).

The second difference between Olve and Kaplan and Norton relates to the perception of the relationships in the strategy map. Kaplan and Norton stress that strategy maps should show the chain of cause-effect relationships (2000, p. 168). Some relationships in a strategy map may, of course, exhibit such strength. For example, if sales per customer increase and the number of customers remains constant, total sales revenues will increase. Petri and Olve define such relationships as definitional relationships (2014b, p. 18). However, these relationships often represent only a small part of the relationships in the strategy map.

The second type of relationships is based on experience. For example, "If we promise shorter customer delivery times, our sales will increase." There is, of course, no firm evidence of this outcome although the company may have internal studies that suggest customer orders might decline if delivery times are too long or that poor delivery performance may result in customers' cancellation of orders. Although the evidence for such relationships may not be conclusive, there may still be the perception that shorter delivery times and orders are related. In fact, even though such relationships are quite uncertain, they are integral parts of the conscious risks that entrepreneurs take in the expectation that the market will reward them.

Finally, the third type of relationships addresses issues that the entrepreneur does not know anything about, but still believes are of value and will drive future performance. No one knows whether they will pay off or not, but all involved are certain that it is worth doing. Petri and Olve talk about these relationships as strategic bets. And as in all gambling, the outcome is uncertain, although some lucky few may reap significant rewards.

The nature of the relationships in the strategy map has implications for the performance indicators in the balanced scorecard. If the relationships in the map are perceived to be causal in nature (as Kaplan and Norton suggest), modelling them requires a meticulous analysis by first identifying them (sometimes this may result in costly investigations of matters that do not have any firm answers, but rather are more of the strategic bet character – i.e. a waste of analytical capacity). Once identified, the strategy and the indicators are, in principle, given. If, on the other hand, the relationships are less certain, the balanced scorecard and the strategy map become tools in the continuing exploration of new opportunities. It cannot be said that the strategy is complete or final. Instead, the use of the balanced scorecard provokes the following question: Should we continue on the current path, or is it time to abandon it and try something new? Petri and Olve (2014b) claim that the strategy map, combined with the balanced scorecard, stimulates a more intellectual evaluation of the strategy-based performance indicators, and thus helps us to see which investments should be continued and which initiatives may be abandoned.

2.3 Strategy maps as a form of visual narration

The strategy map is a visual narration of an organisation's strategy. It emphasises dialogue, the goals and the conduct of activities. The map also legitimises the performance indicators by making the on-going control more strategically relevant.

The elements in the strategy map, plus the creative labelling of its activities and areas, contribute to the map's relevancy and its expressive eloquence. However, something more is often needed for the map to resonate with its intended audience, especially if the users are not familiar with the map's format. The map must present a story, and its narrator must tell that story in a comprehensible and trustworthy way. People (e.g. partners and co-workers) who have never seen a strategy map must understand and trust the story if they are to apply it to their everyday life.

In the next section, we present some elements of good story-telling derived from cinema studies.

2.3.1 Economizing on the means of expression

Developing a personal approach to telling a story with pictures requires a good deal of inspiration in the boundary area between art and science. Edward Tufte, Professor of Political Science, Computer Science and Statistics at Yale University in the United States, described the secret of the narrative picture:

> Graphical excellence is that which gives to the viewer the great-
> est number of ideas in the shortest time with the least ink in the
> smallest space.
>
> TUFTE, 1983, P. 51

It is of interest that Tufte seems to take a minimalist view of documentation. As expected, people who prefer fuller and more specific documentation may be critical of this view.[6] Tufte's point, however, is that simplicity of expression offers more space for richer content. According to Tufte, the secret of the narrative is to economise on the means of expression so that viewers receive the strongest possible experience with the least possible expression. Consistent with his ideas on narrative economy, Tufte also has an abbreviated version of his principle: simple design, intense content.[7]

To illustrate Tufte's principle, we now turn to cinema studies, in which the main focus is storytelling. We can apply this perspective to the strategy map's potential to become a narrative – a story that unfolds. The challenge is not simply to draw a persuasive map – on paper or on a computer screen – but rather to draw a map with much more effect and force by "playing up the map" in an oral presentation. Much can be learned from the history of moving images and the crafting of cinematic narratives.

---

6 See for example Hedberg and Jönsson's (1978) criticism of the too simplistic picture of an organisation's performance in its financial reporting.

7 Tufte defended the short version of his principle by responding in a playful and very knowledgeable way to a reader by deriving the "Feynamn-Tufte" variation of the principle: "A visual display of data should be simple enough to fit on the side of a van". [www.edwardtufte.com/bboard/q-and-a-fetch-msg?msg_id=0001kE].

Steps: (1) Determine at the outstart what tone you want to strike, what effect you wish to produce. (2) Do not put into your story a single word, or action, or bit of description, or character, or *anything* that does not in some direct or indirect way help to produce the effect you desire. (3) Do not omit anything that may help to bring about the same result.

BORDWELL ET AL., 1985, P. 168

The strategy map is not an independent object (the image itself) but rather an integral part of the dialogue conducted in an organisation among those affected by the map's content. At work, when you have a strategy map, you must manage the steps before the strategy map is formulated as well as the steps after the strategy has been mapped in a document (i.e. the systematic and creative economizing on the means of expression). You must first identify the members in the audience (who are influenced by the map and who will influence the map). Then you must choose the right tone so that you can reach them. When the creative selection is completed, it is important to check that you have not missed anything that could make the message (at least) equally strong.

2.3.2 The strategy map in storytelling

How do you apply Tufte's principle – "simple design, intense content" – when you want to summarise a strategy with a map that you can present to your audience and discuss with them? Using the strategy map, you should clarify the simple structure that connects the dimension of time between the four perspectives in the balanced scorecard (i.e. learning and growth, internal business processes, customers and financial results). Actions (drivers) from the lower two perspectives should have effects (outcomes) on the two upper perspectives. This structure lays the groundwork for the strategy map's narrative-friendly format, and supports a uniform way (in a simple form) of linking the descriptions (the rich content) of the company's essential actions and effects in the same picture.

Using the strategy map's simple structure, it is possible to summarise many ideas on actions and effects as partial stories. This summary, however, presents certain challenges, such as economizing on the picture's content while at the same time blending several stories in a simple and useful way.

The strategy map is then presented and discussed at length within the organisation. It is insufficient to simply publish the map on the organisation's Intranet. The map should be presented orally so that the audience can experience it as captivating and relevant.

Because we lack access to organisations' written and oral presentations of strategy maps, we have to look elsewhere for inspiration on how to present a complex message that consists of intriguing relationships. Therefore, we turn to Professor Hans Rosling[8] who is a very successful public speaker thanks to his ability to explain complex relationships using simple and dynamic visualisations. Which elements from Tufte's principle do we find in Rosling's storytelling? We observe immediately

8 We recommend viewing some examples of Rosling's presentations such as these video clips: [www.ted.com/talks/hans_rosling_the_truth_about_hiv] or [www.ted.com/talks/hans_rosling_shows_the_best_stats_you_ve_ever_seen]. Hans Rosling is Professor of International Health at the Karolinska Institute in Stockholm, and is well known for his impressive lectures in which he explains complex development processes using simple visualisations.

QR-links to the video clips (at [ted.com])

that Rosling is very knowledgeable about his topics, which he conveys in a very animated fashion. He knows his story is new and important, and, moreover, he has credible data to support his conclusions.[9] The richness and power of his claims derive from their simplicity, or more precisely – their clarity – both in the data and in the underlying medical, socio-economic reasoning.

Rosling uses many narrative techniques in his storytelling. For example, he turns data and relationships upside down – against people's deep-rooted understanding of how things work and fit together. In the clips referred to in the footnote, he for example challenges the audiences with questions about their knowledge of the world: "How many countries met the definition of developing countries ten years ago? Five years ago? How many meet the definition today?" While the data and relationships Rosling presents are not necessarily new, they seem original because he places them in new contexts and derives new and striking interpretations of them. Similarly, strategy maps, which also present compelling data and describe previously unimagined relationships, may produce new inter-pretations of, say, familiar slogans or traditional visions that the organisations use to describe their goals and activities.

Besides presenting important and credible new data and new interpretations of old data, Rosling's narrative style is imaginative and meticulous as he takes us through the story,

---

9 New, important and credible are the defining features of a captivating, picture-based story. In their best-seller book, *Made to Stick: Why Some Ideas Survive and Others Die* (Heath & Heath, 2007), the Heath brothers make a similar claim. An idea must grab and hold ("stick to") the recipient's attention. Therefore, a message should be designed to pass the SUCCES-test. The message must be 1. Simple; 2. Unexpected; 3. Concrete; 4. Credible; 5. Emotional; and 6. Tell a Story.

step-by-step. He never shows a finished, composite image that requires detailed explanations and interpretations. He lets the image emerge gradually so that the audience has a chance to absorb the content. With this narrative technique, we observe the application of the economizing principle. Rosling uses words and images sparingly in a way that allows his audience to grasp new insights.

To illustrate how the strategy map – step-by-step – can depict a whole range of essential relationships, we can turn to the strategy map that Parks and Resorts Scandinavia (PRS) uses (for more details about this, see Section 2.5). An important principle in their presentation of the strategy map is that the image is presented perspective by perspective. The organisation's simple map structure reveals the pace and order in which it is presented. We believe that this approach to storytelling explains why the strategy map has become such an important basis for joint discussions about goals and strategies among the co-workers at PRS. The strategy map consists of layers of short stories that fit together, without extraneous detail. As the film manual recommends, nothing should be mentioned, or alluded to, that does not directly or indirectly support the intended message of the story.

2.3.3 The story begins with dialogues on how the strategy map should be drawn

How then should such a story begin? A good story always opens with a conflict (or challenge). In its middle section, the conflict deepens unexpectedly. In its concluding section, the conflict is resolved in a way consistent with endings in the story's particular genre.[10] The strategy map can (and should) be used in as many different organisational contexts as possible – such as coffee table brainstorming sessions, group meetings, and managers' roundtable discussions. We return to how the story, step-by-step, is shaped (and formalised) in the dialogue-based composition of the strategy map. Regardless of the context, the map is of most value when the story begins with the organisation's long-term and overarching challenge – the general idea about how the organisation performs its activities.

The story may begin with a presentation of the organisation's goals and key concepts at the highest level. Sometimes the map presents a new interpretation of the organisation's core values. The new interpretation assumes (and requires) a clear introduction. For example, new business plans or change initiatives can be presented in terms of the probable effects of new possibilities or challenges based on one of the scorecard's perspectives (e.g. financial demands, requirements by current or future customers, or other opportunities and threats). The presentation, which should be made in several steps, usually results in a picture that has a number of story lines based on specific activities that are clearly grounded in the development perspective at the bottom of the map.

---

10 For additional reading, we recommend Yates and Orlikowski's (1992) often-cited article on how the genres of organisational communication allow us to recognise and participate in various media forms. They describe how different genres have their own themes and formats that conform to the patterns in social and organisational activities. They exemplify this observation with the genre of the memo, which gradually changed as email technology became available in business. In another case study of major consulting projects, Levina and Orlikowski (2009) demonstrated (with a focus on five different workshop genres) how an analysis can offer insights into the power game that tasks may provoke. They also show how genres can be created and how new patterns of storytelling can be established.

We began this section by emphasizing that a strategy map becomes a living story when the organisation's co-workers use it. Then the map demonstrates its real value. We have also emphasised the idea that people have their own ways of telling a story. This is why we suggest some references to the literature (and some general principles) about storytelling and how it can provide inspiration for everyone involved in the creation of strategy maps.

When is it, then, appropriate to test your own style of story-telling? A natural opportunity arises when you, yourself, get involved in drawing a strategy map. This activity is always a group effort based in a series of dialogues between the people who are comfortable and familiar with the strategy map format and the people who work in the processes that the map presents and explains.

Based on the logic of storytelling, it is clear that an effective strategy map always has a specific audience. Because the strategy map should be treated as a means of communication, you need to identify your target audience. Who are the members of your audience – co-workers, a department, a company, a group of companies, or an external partner? (For a more elaborate discussion about this, see Chapter 3 on how to define the relevant organisation.)

Before we turn to the discussion on how to describe the consequences of digitalisation on organisational activities in a strategy map in the next section, we first offer a summary of a practical manual that deals with the selection of audiences and of perspectives when designing strategy maps. This manual, which is the result of a research collaboration titled Users-Award, presents some strategy maps that describe the goals and outcomes of information systems (Ivarsen et al., 2011b). The box below presents nine steps in the development of a strategy map for an information system. See Figure 2.3 for an example of a strategy map that tells the story of a successful deployment of a new information system.

Nine steps in the development of a strategy map for a new information system

1 *Which information system(s) should the strategy map focus on?*
   The selection is important. Should a new system be purchased? If so, will the changes affect the systems and functions of the organisation as well as its users, customers and partners?

2 *Whose perspective should be taken in drawing the strategy map?*
   Decide which organisational level has the management responsibility and from whose perspective to draw the map.

3 *Who are the participants in the on-going work?*
   Make the following appointments: someone to manage the monitoring; someone to convene meetings; and other co-workers to participate actively in useful discussions.

4 *Be aware of what is already known.*
   The process leader should create a preliminary picture of what has been learned from previous evaluations and follow-ups (e.g. from informal conversations). Then sketch the first draft of the strategy map.

5 *Conduct interviews and/or questionnaires. The data provide the basic information used for the strategy map.*
   Dealing with the data from previous information systems is simple: people who have used another system are entitled to describe their understanding of it. If they are to work with the new system, they should be heard. If people working today lack the type of computer support now available, perhaps there is a similar system like the new one proposed that they can learn from and use in interviews and questionnaires.

---

6 *The first group meeting.*
Agreement is needed on a picture of how a (more) useful information system can benefit the organisation. The strategy map can be used for this purpose. An important goal of the meeting is to interpret the collected data, including the data from the interviews and questionnaires.

7 *Processing the emerging strategy map.*
Useful discussions can provoke ideas and questions of every kind, such as how to improve the monitoring activities (when follow-ups already exist). Before the second group meeting (a few weeks after the first group meeting), the strategy map can be adapted to be more instructive. Goals and other relationships should be expressed as simply and clearly as possible, preferably with key performance indicators associated with the map's content.

8 *The second group meeting.*
At the second group meeting, the documented picture from the first meeting is supported, the evidence for the relationship linkages is confirmed, the incentives and controls related to the use of the information system are presented, the interaction with the system and its development are explained, etc.

9 *Make the strategy map of the information system usable and beneficial in the future.*
The process highlights the advantages of the information system. This process should not, of course, be a one-time exercise. The process, which can be applied to other information systems, should be retained and integrated into the organisation's controls.

Drawing the strategy map is also a group effort. At Step 3, questions are asked about who should participate in the dialogues that shape the story, what the story's central conflict is, and how the story should be told. In Steps 4 and 5, the participants are identified and the data sources for the story are known. Then, when the story's desired effects and its desired activities are established, the storytelling begins. The hope is that in this continuing test of how the map supports the new activities, people responsible for the organisation's strategy will convince their co-workers of its value.

2.4 IT as a strategic theme in the strategy map

In the previous section we demonstrated how strategy maps could be used in order to identify as well as to illustrate the effects of an individual information system. The organisational use of IT should, however, be seen as a something more than just the use of various information systems. Rather, it should be regarded as a consequence of the general digitalisation of companies and of society.

In its basic format, strategy maps allow us to model all types of business strategies – as long as they include the four perspectives of a balanced scorecard (i.e. finance, customers, processes and development). These perspectives generate a balance in time (yesterday–today–tomorrow) and in space (internal–external). This open design has resulted in both positive and negative consequences for users. For managers with a good understanding of the properties of a specific strategy, the basic format is probably sufficiently open for them to illustrate their own strategic choices. However, for managers who are looking for a method that helps them to choose a number of specific strategic priorities, the basic format is perhaps too open. And, it should be said, a strategy map offers no advice on which strategies would be best for a specific purpose.

In order to support strategy formulation, Kaplan and Norton (2001, p. 79) have suggested four strategic themes that can be useful in the process of designing strategy maps. These themes are: build the franchise (growth), increase customer value, achieve operational excellence (efficiency), and be a good corporate citizen (social, environmental and ethical issues).

These themes are too broad to be reflected in just one of the perspectives in the balanced scorecard. In actual fact, they run across the entire map. For example, increasing customer value involves all four perspectives: skills development, smooth internal processes, improved customer service and greater investment capacity.

Likewise, we think that the current digitalisation of society cannot be described only in one of the strategy map's perspectives. Digitalisation, and its consequences, is a strategic theme of its own that runs across all four perspectives in the balanced scorecard and the strategy map.

The importance of IT as it is reflected in strategy maps has shifted over the years. In the early days of computerisation, IT investment mainly concerned the two lower layers: those about learning and growth and those about internal business processes. Gradually, the other two perspectives (customers and finance) became significant.

In advanced nations, the process of computerisation began in the 1960s and was well under way by the late 1970s. At that time, computer technology was primarily regarded as a rationalisation tool. Businesses and governments were hoping for cost savings by automating many administrative tasks such as accounting, invoicing and human resource management. A new organisational unit, the computer department, took responsibility for these automated tasks that were referred to as electronic data processing (EDP).

Investment in information systems was often a time-consuming and costly activity (to some extent this is still true today). New systems required extensive personnel training and sometimes even organisational changes. The computer departments were assigned responsibility for managing the IT investment process, and senior managers often preferred to stay in the background. Insofar as investment in IT was chosen as a theme of strategic study in organisations, the analysis would frequently limit itself to technology choices rather than to strategies for the use of information.

During the 1980s, the vision of IT and its role in business began to change. Academics and data managers began to argue that IT must not be viewed simply as a rationalisation tool, but rather as a technology that had the potential to create competitive advantage and transform organisations. They maintained that the focus of computing ought to shift from cost reductions to revenue generation. In other words, IT might be used as critical business drivers (see for example McFarlan, 1984; Porter & Millar, 1985; Keen, 1988).

A typical example of early IT applications explicitly designed for gaining competitive advantage was computer-mediated communications that companies set up with their customers for order entry. And when companies required customers to use dedicated computer terminals, they effectively created barriers to market entry for their competitors. Likewise, customers considering moving to a competing vendor had to consider extra costs (switching costs) as a consequence of that change. Other examples include the use of sales transaction data in marketing and applications targeted for enhanced service levels. Most important, however, was the potential for companies to capitalise on general improvements in performance and efficiency leading to cost advantages and sometimes even cost leadership.

Initially, a major obstacle to using IT strategically for competitive advantage was not so much related to worries about increasing investment spending. Rather, it had to do with managers' elementary understanding of the potential of this new technology and, subsequently, how it could be used to facilitate competitive advantage. But gradually senior managers understood that innovative types of IT investment could create promising conditions for developing long-term competitive advantage, even if their decisions had to challenge "business as usual" and had to be open for inevitable organisational changes. Or, as James L. McKenney at Harvard Business School put it in 1995:

> The real challenge for most organizations is not technology per se, but the ability to adapt to take advantage of its emerging functionality, which requires both an understanding of how it might function and a readiness to change.

By the early 1990s the new strategic role of IT was widely understood in most areas of business. It was even argued that IT strategies had to be aligned and coordinated with business strategies (see for example Henderson & Venkatraman, 1993;

Falk & Olve, 1996). As a result, the strategic use of IT had to be reflected in all four levels of the strategy map.

With the arrival of the personal computer in the early 1980s and the unforeseen and, it must be said, the unpredictable development of the Internet beginning in the mid-1990s, information technology is now used in every corner of modern society. The proliferation of the Internet has been somewhat spontaneous and has not followed a specified development strategy or master plan.

This chapter was written in August 2016. Conditions for business activity have now completely changed thanks to the Internet, as manufacturers, suppliers, distributors and consumers are all inter-connected and communicating.

Also, during the mid-2000s, a new IT-driven communication culture surfaced which permeates every aspect of our society and our daily lives. Today, social media such as Facebook, Twitter and Instagram are commonplace. The smart phone (beginning with Apple's iPhone in 2007, followed by many others) and the tablet (beginning with Apple's iPad in 2010, also followed by many others) were new phenomena that quickly became new tools both for accessing the Internet and for using a countless number of Apps (applications) specifically designed for these tools. In a very short time, these smart products have become almost as essential as tap water.

It is therefore an inevitable strategic reality that producers and distributors must have a social media presence if they are to reach large groups of their customers and suppliers, and if their customers are to reach them. This reality is just as true for public sector and not-for-profit organisations that need to communicate with their users as it is for businesses that need to communicate with their customers.

What does this situation mean for a company's strategic choices? In terms of strategy maps, the two lower perspectives (processes and development) are still relevant today and will continue to be relevant for the foreseeable future. Here, strategic considerations mainly concern maintenance and development of existing information systems. New developments and innovations are now part of business operations and concern the two top layers.

In our discussion of how information technology has developed since the mid-2000s, we have mainly addressed functions that require IT but are not essentially a strategic issue of concern only to IT specialists and IT departments. On the contrary, to a great extent, IT issues of strategic importance increasingly concern many more people across organisations and thus all the layers of a strategy map. In fact, current IT developments, which we may call a general digitalisation of society, have given us many IT-based tools that are often not talked about as using IT.

The fundamental consequences of digitalisation can be handled in two ways in a strategy map. The first alternative is to highlight the importance of IT clearly in the strategy map's various elements and to emphasise that computers are no longer used only for cost rationalisation and automation. Rather, IT and computers are important parts of the entire strategy (see the discussion above). With this approach, organisations can indicate their specific expectations as far as IT is concerned (in development work, in processes and in customer interfaces).

The second alternative is to ignore the specifics of IT and

instead emphasise the organisational intentions (in which IT is a specific resource, but need not be identified as such).

At the beginning of this chapter, we presented two examples of strategy maps. The map in Figure 2.3 illustrates clearly how IT and its effects can help increase commercial value. In explaining how this is achieved, the assumption is that IT produces positive effects in the process perspective (e.g. "shorter lead times", "more flexible routines", and "lower costs"). These effects are then assumed to generate several positive effects in the customer perspective (e.g. "attract more demanding customers" and "more satisfied customers"). In turn, these effects (as a result of improved IT) increase the customer base, sales and profit, leading to an increasing commercial value.

The strategy map in Figure 2.4 presents a different approach – a strategy map that has no specific IT presence and no specific IT use (it is implicit that the strategy could not be implemented without IT). In the next section, we describe how Parks and Resorts Scandinavia has used this strategy map at both the company level and the Group level. We will now review the role of IT as well as the use of strategy maps in practice at Parks and Resorts Scandinavia.

2.5 Parks and Resorts Scandinavia's strategy map – an example to learn from

Parks and Resorts Scandinavia (PRS) is the largest adventure and theme park group in Scandinavia. It has an annual turnover of around one billion SEK, more than 2,000 employees (in 2015) and nearly three million visitors each year. PRS owns Gröna Lund's Tivoli, Kolmården Wildlife Park, Aquaria

Water Museum, Furuviksparken and Skara Sommarland. PRS reinvests its profits each year and has invested more than one billion SEK in its parks and resorts since 2006.

2.5.1 The Parks and Resorts strategy map

Figure 2.4 presents PRS's strategy map[11]. It shows how the Group and the individual parks (i.e. the entities in the Group) plan to achieve their goals by taking actions consistent with their mission statement. The strategy map shows that the foremost goal is to create a NAV premium[12] (i.e. that the quality and value of the entities in the Group should be greater when belonging to PRS than when being separate entities). Figure 2.4 illustrates this idea with colourful illustrations and balloons for the entities inside the wall, whereas it is greyer and gloomier outside the wall for parks that do not belong to the Group. Figure 2.4 also depicts the Group's financial objectives: profitability and growth. These are the goals the Group must achieve in the long term to be able to make necessary investments in the various parks.

The customer perspective at PRS focuses on guests and visitors as well as corporate customers, travel agencies (that arrange visits and make reservations) and the media (for communications with guests and visitors).

The internal business process perspective focuses on a

---

11 For a more detailed description of Gröna Lund's strategy map and its use of the balanced scorecard, see Petri and Olve (2014a, b).

12 NAV Premium is the opposite of NAV discount (NAV = Net Asset Value) where corporations are traded at a lower price than the sum of the financial value of the operating companies in the portfolio. Parks and Resorts refers to this (in Swedish) as "Substanspremium" (in English: NAV premium).

concept that PRS calls decentralised economies of scale. Therefore, this perspective has two layers: activities that the Group manages, and activities that the parks manage. The parks are responsible for all activities that directly involve the guests and visitors. The Group is responsible for all activities that can be managed centrally. The concept of decentralised economies of scale aims at creating better quality at lower cost. It contributes to achieving NAV premium. Some examples of activities that the Group can manage better than the parks are: financing, acquisitions, joint concept development, administration and public relations.

The development perspective focuses on the areas where the Group can make changes in order to improve efficiency. These efforts aim mainly at improving the quality of the parks (through competence development, systematic quality assurance and joint marketing activities).

In the PRS strategy map, IT is an integral part. Still, the map does not describe IT as a separate strategic area. Instead, this is described in the strategy story (see below): IT is used in the Group's joint competence development, IT is an integral part of all new concepts developed and introduced and IT is essential for the administrative support functions (and thus the possibility of decentralised economies of scale). Moreover, IT provides an important channel for communication and interaction with guests and visitors throughout the entire customer cycle: from planning the visit, via the actual visit, to recalling memories of the visit with photos and films.

The strategy map especially emphasises the vertical relationships (i.e. the relationships between the perspectives). Co-workers discuss the map at staff meetings – perspective after perspective – in accordance with Tufte's principle. When the map is presented, the activities in the development perspective are presented first. These activities may deal with common values and quality standards that are expected to lead to better service and operations in the parks and to the introduction of better attractions at the various facilities (in the process perspective).

New and bold attractions of high quality will provide outstanding entertainment for guests and visitors. Tour operators and travel agents may recommend the facilities, and journalists may write favourably about them. If these groups have positive impressions of the parks, the total number of guests and visitors, and their spending per capita, will increase. In addition, as sales and profits increase, PRS can make additional investments in its facilities.

2.5.2 The development of the Parks and Resorts strategy map

PRS developed its strategy map during the years when Jan Roy (a co-author of this chapter) was the Group CEO and President of Gröna Lund's Tivoli (2009 to 2013). Previously, Jan Roy was an advisor to the President of PRS and the Board, with a special assignment to develop a new business strategy for the Group and its parks. His primary focus was to determine the goals (and vision) for the Group, and to identify strategies that would contribute to achieving these goals. The work required extensive cooperation with the co-workers from different areas of the Group. The overarching goal was to identify how the parks should operate to offer the guests a world-class experience.

In addition to involving the staff in the development of the strategy, Jan Roy also used external consultants for some tasks (e.g. visitor opinion studies). Some were quantitative (post-visit questionnaires) while others were qualitative (e.g. visitor studies of anthropologic character). International studies of trends in the industry were also analysed. Gradually, after much analysis, a strategy and a strategy map were designed for how PRS should design and operate its business.

The Group designed its strategy map based on data from these industry studies, the visitors' opinions, and the owners' financial expectations. Initially, in the years 2008 to 2011, the documentation of the strategy was limited to Power Point presentations that showed the four perspectives in the balanced scorecard in a simple map. However, as the strategy matured, a desire to communicate it more clearly and more widely evolved. An illustrator was hired to redraw the map using more accessible, witty language and cartoon characters, consistent with the Group's hedonistic ideal (see Figure 2.4).

The symbols in the strategy map are drawn in ways to facilitate immediate interpretation of their intended meaning. NAV premium is illustrated with colourful people and balloons within the walls, external financing with an old-fashioned banker in a pinstriped suit, and support to the parks with a perfectionist accountant together with an inspirational coach. These light-hearted drawings helped co-workers communicate about the group's vision, goals and strategies, among both the permanent and the seasonal co-workers. A short strategy story accompanies the graphical strategy map and provides support and inspiration for those who present it to their colleagues.

2.5.3 The link between the Parks and Resorts strategy map and its balanced scorecard

Initially the PRS strategy map was mainly used for educational purposes. It was used to explain how a world-class experience and NAV premium should be achieved, in accordance with the concept of decentralised economies of scale. Gradually, the map also became a way to align the management control system with the strategy.

PRS began to develop the Group's balanced scorecard in the spring of 2011. To show the connection between the strategy, the strategy map and the key performance indicators in the balanced scorecard, thermometers were placed on each of the most important areas in the map (see Figure 2.5). For each

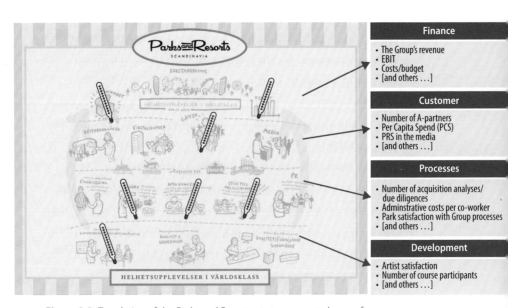

Figure 2.5 Translation of the Parks and Resorts strategy map to key performance indicators in its balanced scorecard (our translation of KPI-names from Swedish to English).

thermometer, a set of relevant performance indicator was designed for the most important areas in the strategy map. These indicators became the most important measures in the Group's planning and monitoring routines. In this way, the PRS strategy map contributes to making the company's management control system more strategic.

2.6 Chapter conclusions

The strategy map is a model and a format that summarises what is most important in the business strategy and helps to illustrate the connection between the strategy and the KPIs in the balanced scorecard. However, the strategy map offers no recommendations on which strategic choices the organisation should make. Moreover, the strategy map does not present a complete picture that can be used to show the organisation's strategy; instead, the strategy map is a simplified picture – a shopping window – of the organisation's most important strategic elements. The strategy map is, so to speak, an invitation to the viewer/reader to take a closer look at the organisation's strategy.

The strategy map's visual representation gives the viewer a quick overview of the organisation's strategy. In some respects, the map's picture is better than its words. The strategy map's compact size also forces its creators to be economical with the explanatory text. Additionally, the strategy map can be read from different directions (top-down or bottom-up).

Yet a picture does not quite explain all the important elements of an organisation's strategy. In addition to the normal strategy documents and business plans, it is also necessary to explain the organisation's goals and relationships in the strategy map – in both oral and written form. PRS, for example, created a strategy story that facilitated dialogue and discussion among co-workers on the most important elements of the Group's strategy. In particular, talking about strategy reinforces its vigour and relevance.

Owing to its flexible format, it is possible to use the strategy map to visualise different strategies as long as they can be sorted in the temporal chronology yesterday–today–tomorrow, using the four perspectives finance, customer, processes and development.

Kaplan and Norton suggest that any strategy should include components from four generic strategic themes. We have identified yet another strategic theme that is relevant to strategy maps: the way the organisation uses IT to digitalise the business. Strategic use of IT, however, does not mean that IT must be explicitly addressed in the strategy map. Maybe even the contrary! The PRS strategy map does not describe IT explicitly. Instead, IT is viewed as an integral part in most of the business processes and relationships. As with other modern companies, IT is an underlying and indispensable resource for its activities at PRS.

The strategy map plays an important role in putting the key performance indicators into a strategic context. Although Kaplan and Norton introduced the balanced scorecard almost 25 years ago as a way to create more balance in organisational planning and monitoring processes, experience to date suggests that their motto, "what you measure is what you get", is not quite exact; the key performance indicators – themselves – are not enough to encourage desired behaviour. Therefore, we think the relevancy of the KPIs needs to be explained and communicated. Traditional financial key performance indicators often have historic legitimacy (because they have been measured previously, the assumption is that they should be measured in the future), while the new, non-financial performance indicators may seem unfamiliar and untested, even unreliable. If an organisation can demonstrate the relevancy of these new strategic key performance indicators, by using the strategy map, it strengthens its strategic management control.

References

Ax, Christian & Bjørnenak, Trond (2005). Bundling and diffusion of management accounting innovations – the case of the balanced scorecard in Sweden. *Management Accounting Research* 16(1), pp. 1–20.

Bordwell, David, Staiger, Janet & Thompson, Kristin (1985). *The Classical Hollywood Cinema, Film Style and Mode of Production to 1960*. New York: Columbia University Press.

Falk, Thomas & Olve, Nils-Göran (1996). *IT som strategisk resurs: företagsekonomiska perspektiv och ledningens ansvar*. Malmö: Liber-Hermods.

Heath, Chip & Heath, Dan (2007). *Made to Stick: Why Some Ideas Survive and Others Die*. New York: Random House.

Hedberg, Bo & Jönsson, Sten (1978). Designing semi-confusing information systems for organizations in changing environments. *Accounting, Organizations and Society* 3(1), pp. 47–64.

Henderson, John C. & Venkatraman, N. Venkat (1993). Strategic alignment: Leveraging information technology for transforming organizations. *IBM Systems Journal* 32(1), pp. 4–16.

Ivarsen, Ove, Lind, Torbjörn, Olve, Nils-Göran, Sandblad, Bengt, Sundblad, Yngve & Walldius, Åke (2011a). *UsersAward2 (UA2) – utvecklad kvalitetssäkring av IT-användning (Slutrapport)*, [www.diva-portal.se/smash/get/diva2:573565/FULLTEXT01.pdf, 2015-12-01]

Ivarsen, Ove, Lind, Torbjörn, Olve, Nils-Göran, Sandblad, Bengt, Sundblad, Yngve & Walldius, Åke. (2011b). *UsersAward2 (UA2) – utvecklad kvalitetssäkring av IT-användning (Bilagor)*, [http://uu.diva-portal.org/smash/get/diva2:573565/FULLTEXT02.pdf, 2015-12-01]

Johnsson, H. Thomas & Kaplan, Robert S. (1987). *Relevance Lost: The Rise and Fall of Management Accounting*. Boston: Harvard Business School Press.

Kaplan, Robert S. & Norton, David P. (1992). The balanced scorecard: Measures that drive performance. *Harvard Business Review* 70(1), January–February, pp. 71–79.

Kaplan, Robert S. & Norton, David P. (1993). Putting the balanced scorecard to work. *Harvard Business Review* 71(5), pp. 134–140.

Kaplan, Robert S. & Norton, David P. (1996a). Using the balanced scorecard as a strategic management system. *Harvard Business Review* 74(1), January–February, pp. 75–85.

Kaplan, Robert S. & Norton, David P. (1996b). *The Balanced Scorecard: Translating Strategy into Action*. Boston: Harvard Business School Press.

Kaplan, Robert S. & Norton, David P. (2000). Having trouble with your strategy? Then map it. Focus your organization on strategy – with the balanced scorecard. *Harvard Business Review* 78(5), September–October, pp. 167–176.

Kaplan, Robert S. & Norton, David P. (2001). *The Strategy-Focused Organization: How Balanced Scorecard Companies Thrive in the New Business Environment*. Boston: Harvard Business School Press.

Kaplan, Robert S. & Norton, David P. (2004). *Strategy Maps: Converting Intangible Assets into Tangible Outcomes*. Boston: Harvard Business School Press.

Keen, Peter G.W. (1988). *Competing in Time: Using Telecommunications for Competitive Advantage*. New York: Harper Business.

Käll, Andreas (2005). *Översättningar av en managementmodell: en studie av införandet av Balanced Scorecard i ett landsting*. Licentiate thesis. Linköping: Linköpings universitet.

Levina, Natalia & Orlikowski, Wanda J. (2009). Understanding shifting power relations within and across organizations: A critical genre analysis. *Academy of Management Journal* 52(4), pp. 672–703.

McFarlan, F. Warren (1984). Information technology changes the way you compete. *Harvard Business Review* 62(3), May–June, pp. 98–103.

Nørreklit, Hanne (2000). The balance on the balanced scorecard – a critical analysis of some of its assumptions. *Management Accounting Research* 11(1), pp. 65–88.

Nørreklit, Hanne (2003). The balanced scorecard: what is the score? A rhetorical analysis of the balanced scorecard. *Accounting, Organizations and Society* 28(6), pp. 591–619.

Olve, Nils-Göran, Petri, Carl-Johan, Roy, Jan & Roy, Sophie (2003) *Making Scorecards Actionable: Balancing Strategy and Control.* Chichester: John Wiley & Sons.

Olve, Nils-Göran, Roy, Jan & Wetter, Magnus (1997). *Balanced scorecard i svensk praktik: ledningsverktyg för strategisk verksamhetsstyrning.* Malmö: Liber

Petri, Carl-Johan & Olve, Nils-Göran (2014a). *Balanserad styrning: utveckling och tillämpning i svensk praktik.* Stockholm: Liber.

Petri, Carl-Johan & Olve, Nils-Göran (2014b). *Strategibaserad styrning: så använder du strategikartor och styrkort för att nå organisationens mål.* Stockholm: Liber.

Porter, Michael E. & Millar, Victor E. (1985). How information gives you competitive advantage. *Harvard Business Review* 63(4), July–August, pp. 149–160.

Tufte, Edward (1983). *The Visual Display of Quantitative Information.* Cheshire: Graphics Press.

Yates, Joanne & Orlikowski, Wanda J. (1992). Genres of organizational communication: A structurational approach to studying communication and media. *Academy of Management Review* 17(2), pp. 299–326.

3. Painting the relevant organisation

ALF WESTELIUS & JOHNNY LIND

A key question in the areas of strategy and management control is the following: What is the relevant organisation? Possible answers: A group of companies? A legal entity, i.e. a company? A business area? A working group/team? An administrative unit or civic district/community? Or does the relevant organisation span boundaries in the way that partnerships of companies and their suppliers and customers do? Is the relevant organisation even a virtual, or imaginary, entity?

Nils-Göran Olve has often addressed this question in his work on the connection between strategy and management control, and the type of organisation – from decentralised organisations to more boundary-spanning entities. Among other topics, Olve has examined management control techniques, but typically in organisational contexts, not in isolation. The importance of connecting strategy with management control and with specific organisational contexts is emphasised in many of his books. Examples include *Decentralisering* (Olve & Ekström, 1990), *Imaginära organisationer* (Hedberg et al., 1994) and *Virtual Organizations and Beyond* (Hedberg et al., 1997). In *Decentralisering*, the connection is evidenced by case studies from Sandvik, Coromant, Mecman and SKF, where the relevant organisation that the strategy and the management control address is a part of a larger organisation. Later, in the 1990s, as in the books cited above from 1994 and 1997, his interest turns towards more boundary-spanning entities – virtual and imaginary organisations.

Olve, clearly one of the believers in the possibility to control, views it as both desirable and possible that those in control paint a plausible and engaging picture of what should be controlled, and whereto. He developed the idea of the imaginary organisation, with an imaginator at the centre, in books, conference papers and articles in the 1990s, often with co-authors, notably Bo Hedberg. At the time, focus on core competencies was a popular piece of strategic advice, and the spread of the Internet inspired a vision of global, electronically coordinated enterprises consisting of constellations of cooperating partners, rather than the traditional legal-unit enterprise concept. How, then, should such new forms of business cooperation work? The Uppsala School,[1] with its notion of relatively stable and inter-connected collaborative relationships between buyers and sellers, served as a backdrop. Their view contrasted with the market-oriented view of business that is based on efficient transactions in competitive markets for goods and services.

Olve was a pioneer in his recognition of the need to develop and exercise control in the more complex business entities that span legal, corporate boundaries (cf. Håkansson et al., 2010). But the time was ripe for such ideas. Olve's writings were contem-

---

1 The Uppsala School's network theory originated in a large European comparative study (set in France, Italy, Sweden, Germany and Great Britain) that examined relationships among purchasers and suppliers in industrial markets (Håkansson, 1982). This study revealed that such markets are characterised by the interactions between mutually dependent companies.

porary with the influential management accounting researcher Anthony Hopwood's call in 1996 in *Accounting, Organizations and Society* for research on information exchange and control in organisational networks and in cooperations that cross organisational boundaries. The discussion of boundary-spanning entities has continued, and now concepts such as ecologies are being employed to determine the appropriate boundaries of the entity to control.

In this chapter, we identify and investigate ideas about what could be viewed as the relevant organisation – the unit to analyse, control and develop. Our investigation involves various worldviews or approaches: network theory, value systems, imaginary organisations and ecology perspectives, each of which emphasises in its own way that every organisation operates in a context. For those striving to exercise strategic management control, this context necessitates paying attention to actors who are external to your own unit – and perhaps even attempting to influence them. We conclude the chapter with a discussion of the development of IT and the international trends in favour of scrutiny, reporting and control that influence the delimitation of the relevant organisation and how management control is exercised.

3.1 Different worldviews, different responses

In traditional business education and financial circles, there is no issue as far as the identification of the relevant organisation to control. An entity exists that must be controlled. In external accounting, this entity is often a company – a legal entity. In strategy, it is a strategic business unit; and in management accounting and in costing, it is a product, or a couple of closely related ones.[2] In the traditional view of the relevant organisation, management control is a key element in defining and delimiting the boundaries. The growth of large corporations, with their hierarchical coordination of activities, has occurred symbiotically with the growth of management control methods such as profitability models, budgeting and variance analysis (Chandler & Daems, 1979).

In this traditional view of the organisation, a clear division exists between market price-based coordination and company hierarchical coordination when the market, with its price-based coordination, is ineffective. This means that management control is used to coordinate the company's internal activities, actors and resources, while the market controls the coordination between companies. What goes on inside the company borders can be influenced by internal control measures; beyond those boundaries, the surroundings are complex and unpredictable.

Organisation theory has raised questions about the appropriate boundary limitations. In classic organisation theory, this is an issue related to the manager's available time and attention (reasonable or possible span of control). Such delimitations are complicated by the institutionalised conflicts between areas of responsibility, provoked by matrix organisations (Simon, 1947; Galbraith, 1971), and from institutionalism ideas derived from sociology, that established traditions and thought patterns

---

2 This unquestioning approach to systemic limitations does not apply exclusively to traditional management control. Other chapters in this book (on the topics of strategy maps, planning, costing and pricing, co-worker control and the controller's follow-up role) also take this approach.

in society control people to a rather large extent. In extreme versions of institutionalism, doubts are raised concerning human agency – whether people are free to select their actions – thus challenging the very idea of management control.

3.1.1 Network theory

The idea that people are limited in their power to exert influence and exercise control was picked up and developed in the network theory of the Uppsala School. According to this view, it makes no sense to limit one's perspective to the organisation as a whole (e.g. Ford & Håkansson, 2006). No person (or organisation) acts freely and independently of the surrounding environment. You always cooperate with others, and others evaluate this cooperation. Therefore, your initiative and individual actions are never self-sufficient; you are always part of something larger. Sometimes, the cooperation is mutual and equal; in other situations, one party may take a dominant or even an authoritarian position. However, even in the latter case, the outcomes are still determined by the interplay (or counter-play). Resources turn into valuable capabilities only through interaction, and interaction builds dependencies, possibly to mutual advantage. The value of your resources will depend on with whom you interact to utilise them. Who you have previously interacted with, and how, will set the stage for present interaction, and will influence who you can interact with in the future, and how such future interaction can be shaped. A consequence for "the relevant organisation" is, then, that it will need to encompass at least parts of the network. However, followers of the Uppsala School, who try not to be normative, are not inclined to recommend such appropriate parts. It is impossible to discern everything, and it is not even clear that a broader perspective will produce better results than a more narrow one.

That the environment influences people and enterprises is not an idea unique to network theory. Classic rationality-based contingency theory prescribes that people should identify relevant factors of importance for potential courses of action. Given a situation's circumstances, better and worse options exist. In strategic management control, researchers have long argued that analyses of the environment are needed. For example, Shank and Govindarajan (1993) highlighted the importance of a company's competitors and its entire value chain in the design and use of strategic management control. In sociologically based institutional theory, what is central is how established norms and behavioural patterns severely limit people's ability to act freely and unconditionally – and perhaps even their ability to recognise alternative courses of action.

In both contingency theory and institutional theory, an identifiable surrounding environment exists – or at least a shared view of the environment. In the Uppsala School network theory, on the other hand, the image of the environment, and the factors that shape that environment, are subjective. There are no objectively accurate images, because actors perceive their world subjectively and act based on their subjective perceptions. In addition, perceptions can change over time – that which at one time seemed positive may at another time seem less so. This relativity makes it more important to try to understand the views of others than to search for an accurate and objective description, as such a description is neither attainable, nor would it lead to improved controllability in a world where people's actions are guided by their subjective perceptions.

From the network school's point of view, agency and control are almost an illusion owing to our limited ability to perceive and understand our complex world. Each actor in a network has a subjective view of the network based on that actor and its network horizon. They can act within their network horizon but are unaware of possibly important elements beyond that horizon. If a network seems new, it is only because we look at a narrowly selected field. Everything is always part of a larger existing web where most components and relations already exist, and everything and everyone (even a start-up organisation) has a history and will likely have a future. Most interactions are not particularly novel. Episodes or critical events, which are both difficult to identify and define, can provide a false sense of causality – that a particular action or event leads to a particular outcome – when the relationships are actually much more multidimensional, and the importance of the identified action is severely overestimated. Effects may also arise not just in proximity, but also at a large social or temporal distance.

Although the companies' embeddedness in a complex web of inter-connected relationships that gradually change over time, highlighted by the network school, make control difficult, management control is not necessarily pointless. Some proponents of management control in such a setting argue it can help companies and their various actors in several ways (Håkansson et al., 2010).

- The first way is to provide a basis for prioritising among the company's counterparts. Management control will then help provide direction for changes in the company and its network.

- The second way concerns the need for management control that captures the indirect effects of the interaction that occurs in direct relationships. Then management control can create a more complete picture of the effects of the various choices.

- The third way, which is closely linked to the previous two, involves how companies and their networks experience constant change as they evolve using temporary solutions. Such solutions are often negotiated where the various actors make certain compromises. The actors accept such solutions because they are temporary and will be in place only until more appropriate solutions are developed. In such situations, management control can help create temporary solutions the actors can live with for the moment.

Basically, the network perspective is related to the increasingly popular ideas about ecology and ecosystems in organisations.[3] We always exist in an extensive network of interactions in which no one has complete control. At least two parties exist in all interactions. Many of our interactions are automatic

---

3 Following James Moore's (1993) article on the ecology of competition in the *Harvard Business Review,* ecology and ecosystems have gained ground in the strategy and management control literature and among practitioners. Whereas Moore and, for example, Iansiti and Levien (2004) are fascinated by situations in which dominant actors sooner or later appear and exert powerful influence, Olve et al. (2013) use business ecology to point to the unpredictable and uncontrollable aspects of cooperation development.

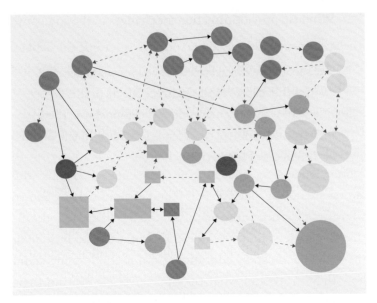

Figure 3.1 Networks/ecosystems. We always exist in a surrounding network of mutual dependence and interaction.

or habitual, and neither novel, creative nor actively chosen. Nevertheless, even when they fall away or change, some day we may recognise that these interactions were, or have become, important (Lundmark & Westelius, 2014). It is impossible to achieve a complete overview or understanding of an ecology or a network – or full control over it.

This insight could lead to abandonment of the idea of control. However, there are people who recognise that the world is complex, but still want to find interpretations and approaches that can provide avenues for action. Olve is among those who sometimes emphasise that there is a point in not seeing everything – or caring about everything. The more limited point of view can provide the will and the power to act by making the world seem simpler and more manageable.

3.1.2 What is a reasonable perspective?

The size of the reasonable perspective is a topic for debate. Westelius (1996) finds that increasing one's perspective has implementation advantages. Yes, the world is complex, our comprehension is limited, and our conceptions are subjective. However, it is for that very reason we, including controllers, should engage in perspectives management by trying to capture, understand and enter into a dialogue with people who at first are not considered central and obvious parties. People who are concerned with and influenced by change (e.g. downstream partners) may be sufficiently important to include in the dialogue. It can be educational and useful to understand how they think and what they perceive. Neglecting their perspectives can create ill will and even a reluctance to make necessary changes. This conclusion is based both on insights about human subjectivity that stretch as far back as Machiavelli (1513) and on the cognitive value of trying to understand other people's worldviews that, for example, Weick (1995) and Boland and Tenkasi (1995) emphasise.

Here, the aim in taking a broader perspective is to design more suitable and more anchored management control. Thus, it is necessary to define which actors should be included in management control activities and which should be excluded. In other words, it is important to create the image of a well-defined organisational entity that includes the actors who are to be directed, and to jointly design a more effective management control structure. Ideally, it would be management control that results in the creation of value for all actors.

3.1.3 **Value systems**

Another approach to subjectivity assumes that it is possible to influence perceptions (Normann & Ramirez, 1993). The point is that customers create value from a number of resources. Therefore, one way in which companies should aim to help customers is by supporting cooperation among the various partners who are needed for the creation of customer value. Such cooperation, a value constellation, is a form of networking. However, in the strategists Normann and Ramirez's (1993) worldview, it is possible to grasp and influence the potential network. The interaction in a value constellation revolves around a reflective actor. The interaction deals with relationships, the co-production of value in value systems, and defining and creating value systems. The goal is to achieve a better match between competencies and customers, and innovation is central: new products, new constellations, and new mobilisations (of resources and cooperation).

In the strategists' mindset, as in the network school, activity consists of interaction, and people's perceptions are important. However, strategy consultants want to be seen as attractive advisors to leaders at (preferably large) organisations. Agency is, then, not an issue. On the contrary, a picture is created of someone who creates value systems and who takes an active role in development activities, even of co-partners. The implication for control is that this active party needs to perceive, assess, and in some respect direct the entire value constellation (the cooperation among all the parties, resulting in a value proposition to the customer). In this situation, management control should aid the reflective actor in orchestrating and directing the network s/he has defined.

Some large car manufacturers employ open-book accounting in their supply chains to create greater knowledge of and insight into the activities in their networks (Kajüter & Kulmala, 2005). With such information, a car company can break down costs for every part in the car and can see how the various suppliers link to each other. This requires a reflective actor who can specify exactly when and how the suppliers provide the car company with information on their activities. This means that the car company develops costing and accounting principles, accounting systems and outlines how the suppliers report this information. It can be noted that the car company alone has full access to all this information, and it is they who coordinate all the activities with the other entities in the value constellation. It is reasonable to assume the car company will prioritise its own interests, and that it uses the information to reduce its costs. But if the car company considers only its own interests, to the exclusion of the suppliers' interests, the suppliers may terminate the relationship. In such situations, it may be quite difficult for the car company to find new, competent suppliers.

The idea behind the value system approach is that cooperation, over time, creates the possibility of developing a jointly created value proposition that can stay competitive. However, cooperation is seldom without friction, and the larger the value system or network, the more possibilities for friction. The more profitable the cooperative arrangements, the greater the possibility to allow all partners to share in the profits and feel that they benefit from the cooperation. In cooperations with poor profitability, there is a greater risk that some party feels exploited.

3.1.4 Imaginary organisations

In Olve and Hedberg's image of the virtual, imaginary organisation, the "imaginator" is the central figure (Hedberg et al., 1994; Hedberg et al., 1997). Clearly, people have subjective images, but like Normann and Ramirez (1993), Olve and Hedberg believe these images can be influenced.[4] To the imaginator, an important part of management control is to formulate an organisational vision, the imagination, in a convincing and captivating way. It is by following the imaginator's imagination that the various entities in the value constellation are mobilised and coordinated as a functional whole – in a legal sense, the organisation is imaginary but in a practical sense, the collaborating units function as one organisation. As in the network school's worldview, the interactions are multidimensional. However, in the imaginary organisation, this does not lead to a questioning of the possibility to direct and orchestrate; rather, the assumption is that the most important aspects can be identified, and that the task is to engage actors in a dialogue regarding those aspects. This multidimensional dialogue is part of the key to getting the units to collaborate, because a give and take in different dimensions can help accommodate the actors' potentially differing goals and ambitions, and develop

---

4 The possibility of influencing people's understanding is also a key aspect of the strategy map discussion in Chapter 2, and the calibration and adjustments of various subjective understandings through dialogue, often related to numbers in reports or targets, is a recurrent theme in other chapters of this book.

a more fair evaluation of their different contributions. Unlike the example of the car manufacturer, the control exercised by the imaginator is not a case of detailed centralism; viewed from outside, the units should perform as one organisation according to the imaginator's imagination, while inside they should work autonomously, but in coordination. This may call for openness and transparency, not least regarding operational data, but the (relatively long-term) contracts between the parties, and their continuing dialogue, should provide incentives that make the coordinated interaction fruitful and sustainable over time.

Examples are available of formalised networking organisations of legally independent companies that join with other companies to create a single, larger entity with clear rules and limits about membership in the organisation (Lind & Thrane, 2005). Such companies are often small, independent companies that join together under a common brand directed toward customers and competitors. Thrane (2004) studied three such organisations in his doctoral research. One organisation was a consulting network of independent consultants. The second organisation consisted of thirteen independent electrical installation companies (employing between 10 and 100 people) that operated under the same brand in Denmark with annual sales of about half a billion Danish crowns. The third organisation was an IT network that consisted of 45 independent companies (employing between 1 and 50 people). In the network, Thane found actors at the centre who maintained a dialogue with the participating companies to achieve a shared vision and management control of the network as a whole. To achieve that ambition, they could not direct the partners in a hierarchical fashion, but needed more openness and transparency to entice the participants to act in the best interest of the entire network. For example, they employed intellectual capital monitoring and follow-ups, visible to everyone in the network, of the various companies' capabilities and competences. Another management control route could be to price goods and services in a way that stimulates cooperation among the participants (Olve et al., 2013).

3.1.5 Ecology perspectives

In ecology perspectives, the field of vision tends to be extended even further. Both Normann and Ramirez' value constellation and Hedberg and Olve's imaginary organisation feature an individual who recognises potential customer value and then orchestrates a product or service delivery that will help customers realise this value. In the ecology perspective of Olve et al. (2013), there is no clear coordinator role.

While certain actors may see themselves as central, other actors may contribute to customer value realisation without being directed by someone else, or even without ascribing to the self-proclaimed imaginator's vision and intended value delivery. For example, leaders at Apple Inc. may see themselves as central to iPhone users' value realisation, but they neither control nor coordinate all the actors whose work contributes to the value iPhone users derive. An app creator may see Apple as a market place rather than as a principal. Or a lecturer, comedian or musician, who tries to reach the public via YouTube, is indifferent to the kind of technical equipment that viewers use. Or a telecom system supplier can train app creators in minimising network traffic so that the telecom system is not overloaded. All of these can contribute to the value iPhone users derive from their iPhone use, without acting on Apple's behalf or request.

This ecology perspective, like that of the network school, asserts it is impossible even for strong players to control all the interactions that produce customer value. Nevertheless, in all entities from the sole proprietorship, via work teams and top management teams at Group level, it is a good idea to complement the attention paid to close-up activities in one's own unit and the direct interaction with partners, paying attention to the interactions those partners have with others, and to the more distant areas of cooperation, interaction and trends in the ecology. Traditionally, a distinction has been made between "internal" control (of a unit or an imaginary organisation) and "external" intelligence. These are not just different terms. They apply to different people or departments with different responsibilities in which external intelligence is usually considered relevant only at the management level – or the business area level.

This distinction is evident in the mainstream research literature on what tends to be termed strategic management control, and can be compared with the management control that can be strategic according to the network school's perspective on strategy (Carlsson-Wall et al., 2015). In traditional strategic management control, senior managers make the important, strategic decisions. They are supported by accounting and intelligence staff who collect financial and non-financial data that describe the company and its environment. This is a process of one-sided information gathering in which the company uses the financial functions and intelligence analysis to collect data on competitors, customers, suppliers and the company's position in the value chain. In contrast with this perception, strategic management control from the network school's perspective consists of the use of information by managers at various levels and specialists in making decisions related to the company's long-term survival.[5] Rather than a central function that gathers information, individuals whose work spans company boundaries in the interaction with key counterparts collect the data. These data, which may be financial as well as non-financial, deal with specific connections to specific counterparts, such as important customers and suppliers. The information gathering is not one-sided; it is important to the company and its actors to disseminate information to key counterparts so that they, too, will be able to spot opportunities for improvement and development that will benefit the interacting companies. The difference between what is traditionally termed strategic management control and management control according to the network school's perspective on strategy, relates to how their proponents view the actors' opportunities as agents. Mainstream research in strategic management control is based in the company's intended strategy, and tends to view strategy as a plan. This can be compared with the network school's perspective, which emphasises that strategy grows from the interaction with key counterparts, in which critical choices are made that effect the company's long-term survival.

The ecology perspective emphasises ever-present but unpredictable change and the difficulty of gaining an overview of the shifting interaction patterns in the environment. Therefore, it is

---

5 The idea that actors at many levels of the organisation participate in strategic management control is emphasised repeatedly in this book, although most authors do not claim they are supporters of the network school.

natural that management control of the area of responsibility, and "external" intelligence, are two aspects required at all levels in order to navigate, act and react strategically. A move towards ecology perspectives may create conflicts between hierarchical levels, between staff and line functions, and between different functional specialisations, as it may challenge established roles. It could also be expected to be adopted and promoted by those who see opportunities to enhance their status or make their work more interesting by moving closer to the higher-status external intelligence, rather than staying locked into traditional management control.

3.2 Powers that control boundary limitations

Today, as companies become increasingly international, value creation is a matter of coordinating internal and external resources. But has this not always been the situation in international operations? The Roman Empire? The British Empire? In past times, delegation of authority and control was necessitated by limited and slow communication possibilities. Today, when we can reach almost anyone, anywhere, at any time in the world, instantaneously (if a connection option exists, at least via satellite), the wish to monitor – and direct – is a force that reduces the local manager's discretion and responsibility. The technical possibilities for transparency and dialogue demand they be used. It may be argued that such technical possibilities would promote greater decentralisation and support a trend toward smaller and relatively more autonomous entities. However, this does not appear to be the case. After the quest in the 1980s and 1990s to demolish the organisational pyramids

3. *Painting the relevant organisation*

and create more agile[6] organisations with smaller divisions, the trend has rather been toward increased and more centralised control. In addition, legislation such as the Sarbanes-Oxley Act (SOX) of 2002 in the United States has increased demands on external accounting and internal control.

The idea that upper management should have a detailed understanding of company activities – via compliance with certified processes and, not least, financial reporting – could be considered a part of the modernity project. As far back as 35 years ago, Feldman and March (1981) observed the signalling value of data collection. In our society, detailed and comprehensive data collection is a symbol of a company's modernity (and competent management), creating a pressure to signal competence by implementing and maintaining extensive information systems. Integrated business systems thus have intrinsic value. Managers tend to be labelled irresponsible and out-of-date if they do not have the possibility to examine operations, including efficiency and profitability, based on detailed data for the entire company.

On the other hand, perhaps management's main focus should not be on the numbers. In his classic study in the 1980s of how senior managers develop networks to create management possibilities, Kotter (1982) presented a human options portfolio. He described how the manager's construction and maintenance of a large personal network of contacts could be used to obtain advice and support when needed. Which strings to pull and which options to call are drawn from a mental

---

6 By agile, we mean manoeuvrable and adaptable.

agenda, that is, an understanding of which issues should be addressed to achieve the desired goals.

Today, more than 30 years later, networking opportunities have greatly increased. For example, LinkedIn is a business-oriented forum for maintaining peripheral contacts that presents potential contact and resource opportunities. Such social networking services are also a form of control. Despite the increased research interest in "the control package", where all imaginable forms of control can be included, it is too soon for a book such as this to analyse such contact networks. Yet we recognise that senior managers' network contacts – and the networks of others in the organisation – are highly relevant in relation to the identification and description of the relevant organisation. These networks have always been part of the informal control of companies' activities. What we now perceive is a gradual increase of the areas where formal management control and monitoring are expected to be used. In some cases, rather one-dimensional control efforts are made by a strong central actor, attempting to scrutinise and influence not only the actor's own organisation, but also its network of suppliers and customers. This can lead to conflict and a sense of lack of trust (Cäker, 2005). In other cases, it is more a case of agreed transparency between somewhat equal partners.

However, in all such attempts to increase the reach of management control, it is essential to create, convey and anchor an image that presents the larger, more boundary-spanning group as a meaningful entity. The entity may be a joint venture, an imaginary or virtual organisation, a network, a value constellation, or a partnership. Because different people may have different ideas about what constitutes a meaningful unit, the dialogue about relationships and boundaries becomes an important and continuing aspect of strategic management control.

3.3 Chapter conclusions

In this chapter, we have demonstrated that the organisational context in which strategic management control is exercised considerably affects the substance of strategic management control. Thus, it becomes important to determine what is to be considered as "the relevant organisation". Traditionally, the definition of the relevant organisation was viewed as relatively unproblematic; the starting point was the company and its boundaries. That which is inside the company's boundaries can be influenced and controlled, while that which is outside its boundaries cannot be controlled, and requires the adaptation of both strategy and control measures. Beginning with the increase in cross-border activities in the early 1990s, this understanding became more complicated, as Olve was quick to identify in the book on imaginary organisations (Hedberg et al., 1994).

When cross-border activities are the focus of control, there are no clear answers to how control should be designed and exercised, to who should control (or be controlled) and to what should be controlled. The answers depend on the worldview adopted; different worldviews offer different answers. In this chapter, we showed this by discussing some different worldviews: the Uppsala School network theory, value constellations and imaginary organisations, and ecology perspectives.

Some worldviews emphasise a focal company and the

potential of its management to act and direct other actors in its environment. This kind of control requires the creation of boundaries around the entity that is the focus of control. The entity may be a company division or department, the company itself, a partnership between two companies, or a constellation of several companies. When entities cooperate, the argument in this worldview is that an arrangement should be created that is favourable for everyone. The collaboration will be dysfunctional if there is just a single winner. This arrangement seems simple if two cooperating companies have no customers and suppliers who may make conflicting demands on the companies.

In other worldviews, the company and its managers may lack the opportunity to control their counterparts. In this situation, control becomes more complicated, and the worldview does not provide clear guidelines on how the companies should act and interact. Then other actors, within and outside the company, can be at least as essential as the company managers for the company's long-term development and its control.

At the same time, it is clear that such views are in stark contrast to international forces that emphasise increased, centralised control by company management. This control takes various forms such as legislation (e.g. SOX) that pressures management to exercise strong control of companies and their various activities. In addition, business journalists, financial analysts, investors, fund managers etc. also ask challenging and detailed questions of management and thereby indirectly exert their demands for control.

The growth of integrated business systems provides company leaders and managers with greater opportunities to increase their company knowledge, as well as greater opportunities for micromanaging control. However, in a world that highly values co-workers' competences, such unilateral control and potential micromanagement may create confrontation and demotivation (see Chapter 6). A central issue is thus how the possibility and demand for more centralised company control will influence long-term prospects for successful development. And those who want to actively manage, or want to activate the collaboration of others in the management, will need to paint a convincing picture of what they view as the relevant organisation to control.

References

Boland, Richard & Tenkasi, Ramakrishnan (1995). Perspective making and perspective taking in communities of knowing. *Organization Science* 6(4), pp. 350–372.

Carlsson-Wall, Martin, Kraus, Kalle & Lind, Johnny (2015). Strategic management accounting in close inter-organisational relationships. *Accounting and Business Research* 45(1), pp. 27–54.

Chandler, Alfred Jr. & Daems, Herman (1979). Administrative coordination, allocation and monitoring: A comparative analysis of the emergence of accounting and organization in the U.S.A. and Europe. *Accounting, Organizations and Society* 4(1–2), pp. 3–20.

Cäker, Mikael (2005). *Management Accounting as Constructing and Opposing Customer Focus: Three Case Studies on Management Accounting and Customer Relations.* Doctoral thesis 933, IDA-EIS, Linköping: Linköping University.

Feldman, Martha S. & March, James G. (1981). Information in organizations as signal and symbol. *Administrative Science Quarterly* 26(2), pp. 171–186.

Ford, David & Håkansson, Håkan (2006). The idea of business interaction. *The IMP Journal* 1(1), pp. 4–20.

Galbraith, Jay (1971). Matrix organization designs: How to combine functional and project forms. *Business Horizons* 14(1), pp. 29–40.

Hedberg, Bo, Dahlgren, Göran, Hansson, Jörgen & Olve, Nils-Göran (1994). *Imaginära organisationer*. Malmö: Liber-Hermods.

Hedberg, Bo, Dahlgren, Göran, Hansson, Jörgen & Olve, Nils-Göran (1997). *Virtual Organizations and Beyond: Discover Imaginary Systems*. Chichester: John Wiley & Sons.

Hopwood, Anthony (1996). Looking across rather than up and down: On the need to explore the lateral processing of information. *Accounting, Organizations and Society* 21, pp. 589–590.

Håkansson, Håkan (Ed.) (1982). *International Marketing and Purchasing of Industrial Goods. An Interaction Approach*. London: John Wiley & Sons.

Håkansson, Håkan, Kraus, Kalle & Lind, Johnny (Eds.) (2010). *Accounting in Networks*. New York: Routledge.

Iansiti, Marco & Levien, Roy (2004). Strategy as ecology. *Harvard Business Review* 82(3), pp. 68–78.

Kajüter, Peter & Kulmala, Harri (2005). Open-book accounting in networks: Potential achievements and reasons for failures. *Management Accounting Research* 16(2), pp. 179–204.

Kotter, John P. (1982). What effective general managers really do. *Harvard Business Review* 60(6), pp. 156–167.

Lind, Johnny & Thrane, Sof (2005). Network accounting. In: Jönsson, Sten & Mouritsen, Jan (Eds.) *Accounting in Scandinavia – The Northern Lights*. Malmö: Liber, pp. 115–137.

Lundmark, Erik & Westelius, Alf (2014). Entrepreneurship as elixir and mutagen. *Entrepreneurship Theory & Practice* 38(3), pp. 575–600.

Machiavelli, Niccolò (2013[1513]). *Il Principe. The Prince*. Milton Keynes: JiaHu Books.

Moore, James F. (1993) Predators and prey: A new ecology of competition. *Harvard Business Review* 71(3), pp. 75–86.

Normann, Richard & Ramirez, Rafael (1993). From value chain to value constellation: Designing interactive strategy. *Harvard Business Review* 71(4), pp. 65–77.

Olve, Nils-Göran, Cöster, Mathias, Petri, Carl-Johan, Iveroth, Einar & Westelius, Alf (2013). *Prissättning: Affärsekologier, affärsmodeller*. Lund: Studentlitteratur.

Olve, Nils-Göran & Ekström, Gunnar (1990). *Decentralisering*. Stockholm: Mekanförbundets förlag.

Shank, John K. & Govindarajan, Vijay (1993). *Strategic Cost Management – The New Tool for Competitive Advantage*. New York: The Free Press.

Simon, Herbert A. (1947). *Administrative Behavior: A Study of Decision-Making Processes in Administrative Organization.* New York: Macmillan.

Thrane, Sof (2004) *The Social and Economic Dynamics of Networks – A Weberian Analysis of Three Formalised Horizontal Networks.* Copenhagen: Copenhagen Business School.

Weick, Karl (1995). *Sensemaking in Organisations.* Thousand Oaks: Sage.

Westelius, Alf (1996). *A Study of Patterns of Communication in Management Accounting and Control Projects.* Stockholm: EFI.

4. Planning for control and evaluation

ERIK JANNESSON & FREDRIK NILSSON

In this chapter, we discuss how management control makes organisations controllable and possible to evaluate. The starting point for this discussion is the idea that an organisation's planning, follow-up and evaluation should help guide it in the right direction (i.e. towards following organisational strategies and achieving organisational goals). The management control literature is much concerned with the design and use of structures and processes that support the formulation and implementation of the organisation's strategies.

It is essential that people in organisations agree on the metrics used, the desired types of decisions, and the distribution of responsibility. In other words, we think that metrics, decisions and responsibility are at the core of the formal control systems we discuss in the chapter. We also discuss control packages and control mixes. They show that in an organisation there are many different control tools that relate to and influence each other in various ways. In the best case, these tools are mutually reinforcing although they may also create tension that makes it difficult for an organisation to achieve its overall, long-term goals. Therefore, the chapter also discusses how what is known as the strategic dialogue can help resolve such tension as well as how new IT solutions influence organisational control and evaluation.

Nils-Göran Olve, whose publications to a significant extent concern how strategic management control should be designed and used, has often focused on organisational control and evaluation. This chapter is based largely on a couple of central publications where he has had a prominent role as author and inspirer. One of these important publications is his co-authored book *Controlling for Competitiveness: Strategy Formulation and Implementation through Management Control* (Nilsson et al., 2011) that, among other things, addresses in detail the concepts of metrics, decisions and responsibility. Taking inspiration from these publications as well as from new insights and experiences of the authors of this chapter, the aim of this chapter is to examine the conditions for control and evaluation. We begin with a discussion of control followed by a discussion of how control relates to evaluation.

4.1 Control

Control can mean a number of things. When we use the term, we refer to the ability to influence the behaviour of managers and co-workers so that they act in ways consistent with the organisation's long-term goals and strategies. This definition closely resembles the description of management control that Robert Anthony presented in the mid-1960s (Anthony, 1965). National and international textbooks of today present control, especially its role in implementing strategies, as a fundamental element of functional management control (see for example Jannesson & Skoog, 2013; Anthony et al., 2014). However, modern definitions – unlike Anthony's original framework from 1965 – emphasise that management control is also used to formulate strategies. With this idea in mind, control and the purpose of management control can be described as follows:

> There are many people who play a part in the success of organisa-tions today: not only the employees, but also people who work for suppliers, retail chains selling the company's products, and other partner companies. How do we involve them in the organisation's work? How do we use their skills and enthusiasm? How do we bring together the efforts made in the various parts of an organisation? Management control provides routines, structures, and processes for all of this.
>
> NILSSON ET AL., 2011, P. 49

As the quotation reveals, an important requirement of manage-ment control is that it supports the decisions of both managers and co-workers. Management control thus includes managers as well as everyone else in an organisation. At the same time, not all management control will give the necessary support – it must be designed to meet the specific information needs of the organisation. As the quotation also reveals, management control deals with how various organisational resources can be used effectively. With this point, we refer not only to financial efficiency but also, for example, to social and environmental efficiency. An organisation's overarching goals determine the kind of efficiency in focus.

Management control, in other words, is a tool that supports decision-making rather than being a tool that top managers use to exercise close follow-up of lower level managers and other co-workers. We are well aware that such a perspective on the role and purpose of management control is normative and reflects a rather harmonious view of how organisations are led. It is therefore important to point out that even though goals and strategies are developed in processes involving co-workers, the board of directors and the senior executives have the ultimate decision-making authority. They also determine how goals and strategies should be transformed into specific plans and then implemented.

However, well-designed management control systems can also be used to achieve short-term goals, even in situations when not all managers and co-workers support them (see Chapter 6). Such management control systems may even be inconsistent with a strong, long-term strategic business approach. In such situations, management control, in the best case, may lead to discussions within the organisation about the suitability of the selected direction. In the worst case, management control may lead to conflict and resistance.

In a classic article, Roberts (1990) discussed the power and effect of management control that aims at short-term financial returns. The article is based on a case study of a profitable British conglomerate (Conglom Inc.) in which control and evaluation were used to stimulate cost focused behaviours among managers and co-workers. Conglom used a decentralised, monetary-focused management control in which its business units were primarily evaluated based on the growth in earnings and the return on capital employed. When Conglom acquired the electric light bulb manufacturer ELB Ltd. – with its entirely different management control style – the Group's senior executives changed ELB's management control system to a focus on the "right things" – that is, on low costs. Furthermore, Conglom divested ELB's businesses that did not fit into its distinctive, low-cost strategy.

This cost-oriented management control system at Conglom resulted in a very strong internal focus on streamlining operations. Growth in earnings and return on capital employed, the two primary measurements of profitability used, soared as a result. However, at the same time, both sales volume and the number of co-workers employed decreased sharply. Some of the consequences of the design and use of the new management control system are described as follows in the article:

> As the cost cutting runs on from year to year, redundancies hit close colleagues and employees with many years service. Skills are lost or left unnurtured. The ground rules become harder to meet as the diseconomies of falling volumes mount. The loss of export markets and the refusal to entertain marginal business seem more crucial. The presentation of an unavoidable period of decline raises questions about the need for a more creative and flexible response to the external world. It creates a desire for a search for positive alternatives rather than an immutable external crisis that necessitates another year of cuts.
>
> ROBERTS, 1990, P. 121

One respondent in the same article said the following:

> It really does require a slightly different philosophy. You don't scrap all the controls or anything like that, but I think you need to be more expansive and outward looking rather than keep on this screw down. If you're going to keep that up for evermore, you can predict that when you get there you won't have a company. You'll lose so much volume, you won't have a company.
>
> IBID., P. 121

A specific and comprehensive management control system that shapes the behaviour of managers and co-workers – in other words, the use of clearly defined and enforced controls – is not always beneficial. The Conglom case study shows that the new control model produced substantial improvement in the financial results. However, as the quotation also reveals, this short-term perspective threatened Conglom's long-term development and even jeopardised its survival. Roberts summarised the negative consequences of the management control system as follows:

> The danger, of course, lies in the possibility that meeting Conglom Inc.'s financial objectives will take a destructive precedence over action designed to secure the long run future of the individual businesses. This is what some managers fear has and is happening within ELB. Rather than blatant asset stripping, they see a conservatism, a reluctance to use corporate resources to attack the market creatively, which for them reflects the dominance of the interests of a Corporate Group who will willingly sell what remains of the business if and when returns begin to fall.
>
> IBID., P. 124

Nevertheless, tight monetary control is not automatically inappropriate. On the contrary, such controls may be quite appropriate in mature industries where low cost is an important competitive advantage. In this particular case study the owners and senior executives seem to have taken the quest for lower costs too far, given that their goal was to create a long-term, competitive business. However, the above quotation suggests that Conglom's owners may not have had such ambitions and were instead prepared to sell what remained of the original company should they become dissatisfied with their returns.

4.2 Evaluation

The previous section emphasises that control assumes a clear understanding of where the organisation is headed and thus what it intends to accomplish. Without careful evaluation, it is very difficult to analyse a strategy's strengths and weaknesses. As a result, learning and development in the organisation are weakened. Therefore, we think management control aimed at developing activities must include an evaluation of performance at the organisational level and/or at the individual level (see Chapter 7 for a discussion of the follow-up meeting where this can take place). Performance that diverges from the selected strategies should be analysed so that action can be taken that is consistent with the organisation's goals. Sometimes, when such analyses reveal that the strategies are inappropriate, new plans are needed. Researchers and practitioners do not find this conclusion either novel or controversial.

It is generally acknowledged that measurement and evaluation influence behaviour (see Kaplan & Norton, 2004; Chapter 2 in this book). It is also well known that management control in organisations may lead to undesirable behaviour that does not advance or support the organisation's long-term development. In some situations, such as in periods of financial crisis, tight and short-term budgetary controls might be necessary and beneficial while in other situations they may cause management to postpone making needed investments. In the latter instance, as Roberts' (1990) electric light bulb manufacturer example showed, tight and short-term budgetary controls may damage the prospects of achieving long-term financial goals. Many textbooks offer examples from research of how poorly designed and/or misused management control have had a negative effect on organisations' long-term goals and strategies (see for example Anthony et al., 2014).

As a result of numerous studies on the various dysfunctional behaviours caused by evaluations, researchers and practitioners have devoted considerable energy to the study of how management control is best designed and used. While these investigations have produced some important and comprehensive insights, it is somewhat disappointing that the general conclusion is that it is difficult to know exactly how the various forms of design and use influence the behaviour of individuals (managers and co-workers).

The reward system exemplifies this difficulty. Consider the following example. Of three co-workers in the same department, one is mainly motivated by the possibility of shorter working hours without loss of pay, the second mainly by financial rewards and the third mainly by increased internal status. The outcome is difficult to predict based on research. In-depth analysis of the factors that motivate the three co-workers is needed.

However, this insight does not mean that it is impossible to establish functional controls in an organisation. Rather, both designers and users of the management control system should be aware of the system's strengths and weaknesses. Among other things, there is today a greater awareness of the importance and power of manager and co-worker dialogues regarding goals, strategies, and results. It is also known that such dialogues should be conducted within a clear framework. Management control offers such a framework in the following two forms:

- structures (e.g. budget templates)
- processes (e.g. budget routines).

At the same time, it is easy to lose sight of the fundamental control principles when an organisation has a complex management control system – i.e. with different control tools used for different purposes and in different ways.

In the next section we present three important concepts to keep in mind when developing and using management control: namely, metrics, decisions and responsibility. Thereafter we discuss the importance of these concepts when creating a strategic dialogue. We then examine different control models and their roles in a strategic dialogue before concluding with reflections on how new IT solutions can facilitate control and evaluation.

4.3 Metrics, decisions and responsibility

One way to create organisational control is to focus on the concepts of metrics, decisions and responsibility when management control systems are designed. Both researchers and practitioners are very familiar with the three concepts. Nils-Göran Olve, among others, has used these concepts to address, in pedagogic fashion, control and evaluation. In *Controlling for Competitiveness: Strategy Formulation and Implementation through Management Control* (Nilsson et al., 2011), Olve and his co-authors use these concepts to discuss "how management, and above all the controllers, ensures that strategies impact on day-to-day activities" (Nilsson et al., 2011, p. 173). In this section we present an overview of these concepts based on the discussion in the book by Nilsson et al. (2011).

4.3.1 Metrics

Metrics, which communicate a specific attribute about the measured object, can be presented in both numbers and letters. If the measured object is the organisation as a whole, return on total capital is a commonly used metric that is expressed in numbers. If the measured object is instead the competence of the organisation's co-workers, the metric may be expressed in words (e.g. inadequate, satisfactory or very good). In choosing a metric, the selection process should be based on the organisation's strategy. However, there might be other reasons for choosing a specific metric, for example to create organisational legitimacy or to draw attention to the organisation's particular area of accomplishment or expertise. Catasús (2013) explains the use of metrics to establish legitimacy as follows:

> One can also imagine that organisations try to reduce the risk of being thought of as "improper" by imitating organisational heroes or their colleagues and by producing key performance indicators – because "everyone else does it". One possible reason for the production of key performance indicators is thus the quest for legitimacy. However, it is seldom (if ever?) the case that management explicitly describes the purpose of its use of key performance indicators thus: "We do it because everyone else does it, and we want to be as modern as everyone else". It is, however, acceptable to make a

rational claim for the production of key performance indicators which are not used (e.g. "The company has a greater likelihood of survival"). However, such a claim is scarcely functional. This way of justifying the use of key performance indicators can be called the *legitimacy purpose.*

CATASÚS, 2013, PP. 147–148, EMPHASIS IN THE ORIGINAL; TRANSLATED FROM SWEDISH

Petri and Olve (2013), among others, have discussed the quest for legitimacy as a powerful motivator when management decide which metrics to use. On the whole, the quest for legitimacy is one explanation why organisations have a tendency to be increasingly alike – we usually call this tendency isomorphism (see for example DiMaggio & Powell, 1983). Because isomorphism may weaken the alignment between the unique strategy of the organisation and the management control system, it is important to highlight that there is not an obvious set of metrics that should be used (cf. Nilsson & Stockenstrand, 2015). The metrics should be carefully selected based on how well they communicate the strategy and how they influence co-workers' behaviour. Furthermore, the costs of collecting relevant data should be considered. The marginal benefit of the "perfect," although costly, metric may be low relative to the next best, and far cheaper, option. According to Nilsson et al. (2011), one can categorise metrics on three levels:

- Metrics linked to financial reporting (Level 1)
- Financial-analytical metrics (Level 2)
- Non-financial metrics (Level 3).

Level 1 metrics, derived from the organisation's accounting records, relate to specific amounts (i.e. from the balance sheet and the income statement) or to a combination/calculation of several such amounts. Examples include operating profit and profit margin. Financial-analytical metrics (Level 2) also have a financial origin, but some information used is not from the accounting records. Present value calculations and cost per customer visit are examples of such metrics. Examples of non-financial metrics (Level 3) are acceptable product quality levels, delivery precision and number of patents awarded. Such metrics are used when Level 1 and Level 2 metrics are not assumed to express desirable behaviours in a sufficiently specific manner (i.e. related to operations). Level 3 metrics are therefore common, at least in the design of the management control system. When it comes to the use of these metrics, the risk is that people only pay attention to them when warranted by a particular financial situation, i.e. when the results of Level 1 and/or Level 2 metrics are on a satisfactory level. The idea that positive outcomes from Level 3 metrics should lead to long-term positive, financial outcomes seems to be forgotten when the financial situation weakens. A manager at a large Swedish company stated the following (in an interview with one of the chapter's authors, translated from Swedish):

> I would never renounce hard numbers. One cannot claim, when we have achieved 4.5 [on a scale of 1 to 5] on customer satisfaction but not yet earned any money, that the customer rating makes up for it. No, that doesn't work.

Another way to discuss metrics is to divide them into two categories: *leading* and *lagging* metrics (Kaplan & Norton, 1996). Leading metrics – sometimes called performance metrics (or performance drivers) – communicate concrete, desirable actions in the here and now. They are supposed to drive a specific behaviour, for example via metrics such as the number of sales meetings per week or the number of training days per year. Thus, leading metrics indicate what management think is important to implement the formulated strategy. Later in the chapter, we return to this idea in a discussion on strategic betting.

The essential use of lagging metrics – sometimes called outcome metrics – is in linking them to leading metrics. For example, the staffing level (a leading metric) is used to reach a high level of customer satisfaction (a lagging metric). Other examples of lagging metrics are return on equity and the number of workplace accidents per time period. A feature of lagging metrics is that they do not in themselves communicate desired behaviour – the outcome of the metric can be achieved in several different ways. Rather, lagging metrics have a more long-term focus aiming at successfully implementing the chosen strategy.

Leading metrics can therefore be used to determine how lagging metrics are likely to develop. Used in combination, the two types of metrics provide a more nuanced assessment of organisational performance, in relation to the chosen strategy, than either of the two used separately. The strategy map, originally developed by Kaplan and Norton (2004) and discussed in Chapter 2, is a pedagogical tool that graphically illustrates the relationships between an organisation's leading and lagging metrics.

Scania is a Swedish company that attaches great importance to the choice of metrics it uses to explain how it creates value for its customers and thereby for its owners:

> *Metrics* are very consciously selected to communicate strategic priorities. New metrics can be introduced and old ones retired if Strategic updates make it desirable to do so. The metrics used are clearly derived from a communicable "story" about what will make Scania successful. This story starts with the idea that life-cycle profitability for customers should be higher if they own a Scania truck rather than a competing brand. It can be contrasted with strategic stories in some other firms, which start from ideas of producing financial benefits for corporate owners, and comparisons with competing firms. Obviously these matter at Scania as well, but the company seems to have been successful in communicating benefits to customers as the driving force for all activities.
>
> OLVE, 2014, P. 103, EMPHASIS IN THE ORIGINAL

An important conclusion Olve draws in the case study is that Scania's management control system – in particular, how metrics support decisions and are connected to responsibility – is a major reason for the company's strong competitive advantage. Because this case study gives us a unique insight into one of Sweden's most successful and well-managed manufacturers, we offer more examples from Scania later in this chapter.

4.3.2 Decisions

The fact that metrics are of great importance when managers and co-workers make decisions is seldom questioned. Since decisions and actions affect the entire organisation, the organisation's strategy should be considered when decisions are made and metrics are selected. However, the reality is that many decisions are made independently of the metrics used. Personal preferences or pure gut feelings are not uncommon in decision-making. It is therefore a common expectation of the people who select an organisation's metrics that these metrics will communicate what is important in the organisation in a reasonably clear way so that the message – consciously or unconsciously – reflects the particular decision-maker's situation. As previously noted, it is not entirely clear how the design and use of the management control system influence the behaviour of managers and co-workers – and thus the decisions they make.

Scania has tried to address this challenge by emphasizing the importance of making decisions supported by metrics linked, directly or indirectly, to a well-thought-out method – for example by paying attention to and learning from variances.

> *Decisions* at Scania involve methods, capacity, investments and delivery value, for example. For all of these there seems to be a coherent approach to decision-making, where shared key metrics play an important role in structuring motives and priorities – always based on strategy. Reacting to deviations also belongs here. Procedures and instructions are simple and highly decentralised, but intended to ensure that metrics receive sufficient attention when it matters – e.g. that deviations are resolved.

Of particular importance here is the way in which decision-making is embedded in methods. Having learnt from the Toyota way in the 1990s, Scania controllers claim that if the prescribed methods and SPS [Scania Production System] are practiced correctly, success should follow.

OLVE, 2014, P. 103, EMPHASIS IN THE ORIGINAL

4.3.3 Responsibility

Another consideration in the selection of metrics and the distribution of responsibility is that decisions have different time horizons (i.e. decisions have consequences for different time periods). Decisions with long-term consequences are usually called strategic decisions, decisions with a time horizon of one year or less are usually called tactical decisions, and decisions that affect daily activities are called operational decisions.

However, it is important to understand that even tactical and operational decisions may have long-term strategic consequences. The managers and co-workers who are close to the market and to the competitors – for example, in customer meetings or in product assembly and delivery – are the people most distant from the centre of the organisation. For this reason, many organisations delegate many decisions to the operational level because they are well aware of the importance of those decisions for tactics and strategy. At the same time, this has major implications for the design and use of the management control system. One clear implication relates to how responsibility is distributed and evaluated.

> *Responsibility* is a key aspect of management control. If there is
> a well thought-out division of responsibility in the organisation,
> employees will always be focused on what is currently considered
> important, and there will be less risk of important questions falling
> between two stools. Responsibility can lie with individuals, groups
> or organisational units.
>
> NILSSON ET AL., 2011, P. 177, EMPHASIS IN THE ORIGINAL

Responsibility is communicated with the help of metrics. For example, the use of profit margins to evaluate a business unit signals that the unit is responsible for the organisation's income statement and is expected to find the relevant means to achieve stated goals. Responsibility thus deals with specifying what managers and co-workers are expected to influence and thus how individuals and organisational units will be evaluated. In other words, responsibility assumes that people can influence – make decisions about –the activities that the metrics reflect.

The specificity of responsibility varies depending on which metrics are used. If the metric is the above-mentioned profit margin for a business unit, this gives people with responsibility for that measurement considerable flexibility in choosing how to reach the margin. If the metric is instead the number of performance reviews conducted annually per unit manager, the managers only have a single option to reach the stated target: to conduct the requested number of performance reviews.

However, distributing responsibility with the help of metrics is often easier said than done. The literature contains many examples of situations in which the responsibility is greater than the associated authority. For example, it may not be possible for the manager who will be evaluated to affect the metric. Or the metric does not link to the organisational strategy. Nevertheless, there are good examples of the opposite situation. Scania is one such company:

> *Responsibilities* are based on forecasts that are updated each quarter, and on the structured approach to continuous improvements at all levels of organization. Methods (in particular SPS) and living according to Scania values are rewarded with bonuses, which are linked to non-financial metrics for most employees but to financial outcomes for senior executives. Targets are downplayed, or at least reinterpreted as a continuous quest for improvements. Where the tasks of an organizational unit or a specific employee in other organizations might be expressed in terms of financial targets (a budget), Scania controllers refer instead to following methods in an appropriate way and thereby achieving improved performance.
>
> OLVE, 2014, PP. 103–104, EMPHASIS IN THE ORIGINAL

In sum, we conclude that both strategies and management control systems cannot be overly rigid and restrictive in their design and use. It is essential to have space for flexibility and adaptability when changes in the business environment and in organisational activities occur. Above all, it is important for managers in decentralised organisations, characterised by rapid change, to continually evaluate which metrics should be used, to review which decisions are important, and to examine how responsibility should be distributed and evaluated. At the same time, there are challenges with undertaking such actions, especially when resources and time are limited, as they inevitably are. In the next section we discuss a dialogue – the strategic dialogue – that is useful for meeting such challenges.

4.4 The strategic dialogue

The strategic dialogue means simply that senior executives as well as co-workers at the lower organisational levels have the opportunity to evaluate the organisation's strategies and identify new and possible strategic directions. The strategic dialogue is intended to establish a forum in which strategies can be critically examined and re-examined. Furthermore, the design and, above all, the use of management control influence these dialogues. Robert Simons (1995) argues that although most management control systems have a relatively similar design, the distinguishing feature of each is how it is used. He has identified four levers of control (Ibid. p. 7), all of which are needed in a control model and are meant to interact:

- *Beliefs systems*: Aim at assuring that the organisation's core beliefs will provide support and direction in the search for new opportunities.
- *Boundary systems*: Aim at limiting risk-taking in the search for new opportunities.
- *Diagnostic control systems*: Aim at evaluating the implementation of the intended strategies.
- *Interactive control systems*: Aim at facilitating organisational learning and the formulation of new strategies.

We focus on the last two levers because they have a particularly strong connection to the concepts of metrics, decisions and responsibilities.

The middle two arrows in Figure 4.1 help us understand *diagnostic control systems* (we discuss the two outermost arrows below). The control process begins when top management send information to the co-workers at the lower organisational levels about the organisation's strategy (second arrow from the left). This information includes the metrics that should be used to make decisions and how responsibility should be distributed and evaluated. The co-workers use these metrics to provide management with continuous updates on operational performance in connection with the intended strategy and plans (third arrow from the left). Top management evaluate this information and inform the lower organisational levels whether performance is consistent with the strategy or if further action is needed (second arrow from the left).

Because the diagnostic control system takes strategies largely for granted, deviations from plans mean that additional efforts are required to make sure that the plans are actually implemented. For example, if the sales department has not achieved its target of sales visits per week, the department will very likely be requested to increase its sales visits. If strategies and goals are changed, the change is made after decisions by senior executives.

The interactive control system has the same components as the diagnostic control system (the middle two arrows in Figure 4.1). However, interactive control systems have another central feature – the chosen strategy is continuously re-evaluated and is not taken for granted. This part of the interactive control system is based in the far right arrow and in the far left arrow in Figure 4.1. In addition to following up on the chosen strategy, top management provides co-workers at the lower levels with information on the strategic domain. This means that management tries to identify the uncertainties that

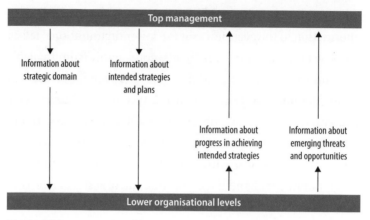

Figure 4.1 Representation of Simon's (1995, p. 6) framework that clarifies the difference between diagnostic and interactive control systems.

characterise the chosen strategy, such as competitors' possible future actions and customers' possible changes in preferences. Co-workers who are closest to the market should have a good understanding of expected or possible market changes. Thus, they can provide information about threats and opportunities. Based on this information, as well as information on company performance in relation to the intended strategy, management and co-workers can have a dialogue about the strategic direction. This dialogue can lead to new insights on how to modify the current strategy or to a decision on a new strategy.

So how often should organisations have the latter type of strategic dialogues? Ideally, these dialogues should be on-going, at all times, with the consequence that strategies and metrics can be revised at any time. In practice, however, this is challenging because more energy is required from the organisation than may be available. Long-term, persistent efforts are therefore needed to learn how the organisation can achieve the right energy level. However, few organisations actually succeed in pushing this agenda. Typically, organisations find it reasonably satisfactory to conduct a "sufficient" number of dialogues.

While both diagnostic control systems and interactive control systems create openings for dialogues on current strategies, only the interactive addresses the strategic dialogue seriously with its clear affirmation of new strategic opportunities. On the other hand, a diagnostic control system is the core of planning and follow-up aimed at achieving control based on evaluations. Therefore, it is important to point out that not all management control should automatically be interactive. In reality, there are probably very few examples of situations in which a single control tool is used exclusively in either a diagnostic or interactive manner. It is much more common that a control tool is used both diagnostically and interactively and that the focus on one of them changes depending on the situation.

As an example, consider a manufacturer with a clear differentiation strategy. Because an important part of its business strategy is climate neutrality, the company compensates for the harmful environmental effect of its operations by making external environmental investments. The aim is that its total effect on the environment is, at least, zero, and preferably positive. Thus, the company declines to compromise on certain areas (e.g. specific budgeted costs) in the dialogue on the implementation of its strategy. For example, with regard to budgeted costs for carbon emissions reduction, the company constantly monitors that relevant resources are used as planned (diagnostic control). Conversely, for other budgeted costs the company may find that dialogue is advantageous – such as a dialogue on the costs of co-worker training facilities. Senior executives do not regard it as important that such costs are held strictly to budget. In this case, the dialogue centres on the relevance of the target for the strategy (interactive control).

Most organisations use diagnostic control in a way that emphasises that metrics should reflect important decision areas as well as the distribution and evaluation of responsibility. As discussed previously, this type of management control can, however, lead to undesirable behaviour because of the difficulties in linking the management control's design and use with the desired outcome – not least because the strategies may require change. In such situations, metrics, decisions and responsibilities in the diagnostic control system need to be supplemented with information that can provide new insights on how activities should change in order to maintain competitive advantage.

In the next section we describe how the structures and processes of management control have changed and developed against the background of the need to support both strategy formulation and implementation. Our discussion so far shows that the earlier dominance of budgetary control, originally viewed mainly as a diagnostic control tool until Bergstrand and Olve (1981), among others, pointed out the advantages of interactive budget use, has been complemented with other types of control tools that, to an even greater degree, are based on interactive control ideals with the strategic dialogue at its centre. This development and its consequences are described in the next section.

4.5 From budgetary control to the control package

What should the strategic dialogue focus on? In other words, which control tools are the starting points in the dialogue? Although we offered some suggestions in the previous section, generally speaking the answer depends on each organisation's particular situation. Nevertheless, the last 40 years have witnessed a systematic shift in opinion on this question. Until the 1980s, the starting point was largely the financial metrics and the budget. The budget was regarded as a plan in financial terms. It is also reasonable to talk about different types of budgets – operating budgets, budgeted balance sheets and budgeted cash flow statements. The budget was, and still is, an important part of many organisations' management control system. However, because the budget is built around specific forecasts, critics claim the budget risks becoming unusable in rapidly changing environments (Wallander, 1994).

It is not only budgets that are debated and criticised. Towards the end of the 1980s, in their book *Relevance Lost: The Rise and Fall of Management Accounting,* Thomas Johnson and Robert Kaplan (1987) presented an analysis that has had significant influence on the development of the subject area of management control and its practice. This book, without doubt, was the beginning of a trend reversal in how control tools were designed and used. The authors made a convincing argument that management accounting was too late to be of use, too aggregated, and too accounting-oriented. As a result, they argue, management accounting had lost its relevance as a support for strategic, tactical and operational decision-making. The authors, who set their book in the American business milieu, claim that, among other things, the capital markets' short-term perspective and the demands from financial accounting to a very great extent influence management accounting. (See Nilsson & Stockenstrand, 2015, for a detailed discussion of the connections between management control and financial accounting.) Johnson and Kaplan's book created a lot of debate among practitioners and researchers in the United States and in Europe.

One of the control tools introduced as result of the "Relevance Lost" debate was the balanced scorecard. This control tool, which has enjoyed widespread popularity throughout the world, is the subject of an impressive number of books and articles. Two well-known examples of such books are *Performance Drivers: A Practical Guide to Using the Balanced Scorecard* (Olve et al., 2000) and *Making Scorecards Actionable: Balancing Strategy and Control* (Olve et al., 2003). Two more books on the balanced scorecard were published in the Scandinavian market in 2014: one for academics (Petri & Olve, 2014a) and one for practitioners (Petri & Olve, 2014b). Chapter 2 in this book describes the balanced scorecard in detail with special emphasis on what is termed the strategy map.

The balanced scorecard's history began with the now classic article by Robert Kaplan and David Norton, "The Balanced Scorecard: Measures that Drive Performance", that appeared in the *Harvard Business Review* in 1992. In the article, the authors present four perspectives that are fundamental to the scorecard – the financial perspective, the customer perspective, the internal business perspective and the innovation and learning perspective – and describe the relationships between the perspectives. They claim that, because no perspective is more important than another, a balance is needed among them. Each of the four perspectives contains a number of metrics that communicate overall strategic direction. The logic is that the metrics in the last three perspectives focus on what needs to be done to achieve a desirable financial outcome (i.e. metrics in the financial perspective).

In the discussion on which metrics to choose, a useful concept is strategic betting (see for example Petri & Olve, 2014a, b). This concept deals with the design and use of appropriate metrics that can achieve overall objectives. Betting gives the strategic dialogue, about which areas in the strategy to focus on, a central function.

4.5.1 The control package

In the 2000s, the discussions on control began to deal increasingly with the relationship between various control tools or, more specifically, with what is referred to as the control package. Malmi and Brown's (2008) framework was the starting point for many of these discussions. Figure 4.2, which presents this framework, proposes that control tools are of various kinds. Administrative controls, which is in the bottom row of the framework, deals with the governance structure and organisational structure as well as with the policies and procedures that specifically clarify which behaviours are desirable.

The centre rows of the framework (Figure 4.2) deal with what are commonly regarded as formal planning and monitoring. That includes planning of a more comprehensive character with both long-range planning and action planning, as

Cultural controls			
Clans	Values		Symbols

Planning		Cybernetic controls			Reward and compensation
Long-range planning	Action planning	Budgets	Financial measurement systems	Non-financial measurement systems	Hybrid measurement systems

Administrative controls		
Governance structure	Organisation structure	Policies and procedures

Figure 4.2 Representation of Malmi and Brown's (2008, p. 291) framework for management control systems.

well as budgets, various measurement systems, and reward and compensation.

Considerable research has been conducted on the relationship of these control tools in which the concept of integrated control is an important starting point. With integrated control, the assumption is that a company's planning and follow-up systems have the same design and use at all organisational levels (Jannesson et al., 2014, p. 2). The purpose of integrated control is to create a consistent focus in the organisation on what is important, and thereby to increase its potential to achieve a strong competitive advantage.

A number of detailed, longitudinal case studies (e.g. Atlas Copco, Saab AB and Scania) emphasise the importance of the creation of integrated control as well as of clearly linked strategies (i.e. strategic congruence). In these cases, a high degree of integrated control and strategic congruence has contributed to the companies' competitive advantage.

The top row of the framework (Figure 4.2) deals with cultural controls that consist of clans, values and symbols. Cultural controls are at the top of the framework to emphasise that they change slowly and have a large influence on how the other control tools develop.

Malmi and Brown's framework shows that a number of different control tools can be used to influence behaviour. However, these authors do not comment on either a desirable or a most-used combination of these tools. In practice, we find that many organisations use a large number of such tools. Åkesson and Siverbo's (2009) recommendation that care should be taken to avoid overdosing on the use of control tools is therefore warranted (see Chapter 6). They find that while new control tools are often added to the existing package, old control tools are rarely removed. In their opinion, this situation can increase the lack of clarity in the overall message that control tools are intended to send. When many different messages are sent from various sources, confusion may be the result.

4.5.2 The control mix

The control mix is another way to think about control packages and the possibility of an overdose of controls (as observed in the previous section). Based on Nilsson et al.'s (2011) detailed discussion on the control mix concept (that they consider almost identical to the control package), the control mix deals with the following:

- which control tools should be used and how
- which control tools should have a more or less prominent role in the management control system
- how the chosen control tools should relate to each other.

In this connection it is important to note, however, that the control mix is not a new concept. For example, more than thirty years ago David Otley (1980, p. 424) expressed very similar ideas. He observed that the accounting information system is included in a control package together with several other control tools.

Fundamentally, the control mix is about creating an awareness of which control tools in an organisation send which signals, as well as an awareness of their consequences (alone or in combination) for organisational behaviour. This awareness is a key factor in creating control. Failure to understand this can lead to significant problems.

We can take an organisation with strong cultural controls as an example. When managers do not understand how strong the cultural controls actually are – this lack of understanding has important behavioural implications – the organisation may try to use formal planning and follow-up to achieve behavioural change that to a certain extent conflicts with the signals the cultural control sends. In all likelihood, this will not cause a behavioural change because the signals from cultural control are considered prioritised. Time and energy have then been spent trying to achieve a change that was probably doomed to failure from the start. A better awareness of the strength of the cultural controls would probably have resulted in a greater chance of achieving the desired behavioural change.

In fact, many examples exist of how organisations deliberately send conflicting control signals using various control tools. Their purpose is typically to achieve "the best of two worlds", for example, by encouraging business entities to cooperate so that individually they perform as well as possible.

The management control at the Swedish aerospace and defence company, Saab AB, is a good example (see for example Jannesson, 2014). Around the year 2003, Saab devised a new corporate strategy aimed at creating "one Saab", that is, a company in which, among other things, synergy realisation was central. To achieve this change, management control was changed significantly. In terms of Malmi and Brown's (2008) framework, the changes applied mainly to the organisation and governance structures, planning, and cybernetic control (tactical planning and follow-up with a time horizon of one year). The organisation and governance structures were changed by locating similar operations in the same business unit, by grouping related business units into segments (a form of comprehensive business areas), and by creating horizontal groups of managers from different business units. Planning changed by introducing a Group strategic process in which business unit managers participated in the discussions on the corporate strategy. Regarding the cybernetic controls, the use of budgets and metrics was primarily changed, among other things, by emphasizing the importance of increased cost efficiency so as to create resources for synergetic business opportunities.

These control tools in combination sent signals consistent with the Group's critical success factors. However, the Group used other control tools for the primary evaluation of the business units: financial metrics. This meant that the business units to a considerable extent prioritised their own activities in order to achieve these financial objectives. Among the various consequences, two in particular were noteworthy. The back-and-forth discussion on ownership of the costs and revenues in business transactions that crossed unit borders increased. And similar platforms in various business units were developed independently rather than as one central platform located in a single unit.

The outcome of Saab's conflicting control mix was that the business units acted in accordance with both dimensions – they cooperated with each other at the same time that they prioritised their own activities – but without the Group realising the full benefits of either. In particular senior executives wanted a greater degree of synergy realisation within the entire Group.

As the Saab example shows, the essential and basic principle behind the control mix is that it should be a deliberate mixture of control tools and signals. Striking the right balance between the two, however, is not easy. There is no simple recipe for how to achieve this balance. For this reason, much of the strategic dialogue should deal with the design of the control mix. As observed above, such dialogues should address these three aspects:

- which control tools should be used and how
- which control tools should have a more or less prominent role in the management control system
- how the chosen control tools should relate to each other.

The dialogue should also involve the understanding that the use of existing control tools may well mean that the desired results of the control mix may not be realised, either partially or completely. Therefore, Malmi and Brown's framework is useful because it identifies several commonly used control tools. Using this framework, it is possible to analyse the organisational roles of the various control tools and how they interact with, or counteract, one another.

In the next section we discuss a support tool that can be used in these discussions: the organisation's IT system.

4.6 IT as enabler

The popularity of the two concepts – control packages and control mix – increasingly reflects a strong desire among organisations to take greater control using integrated control systems. This desire for plans and follow-up is especially notable at complex organisations with their many units and hierarchical levels. The need to make metrics, decisions and responsibilities clear is significant because of the high degree of decentralisation that is typical at such organisations.

Organisations need structures and processes that can facilitate rapid decision-making and, to some extent, informal management control. Even strategic dialogues, with their challenging and probing character, require a structure that permits the formal exchange of information – at least at complex organisations where it is not always possible to conduct this type of dialogue informally. As we have previously stated, the management control system has an important role in this context. Large, complex organisations implement various IT solutions for the collection, collation, analysis and distribution of management control information (see for example Lindvall, 2009, for a description of how new IT influences the controller's role).

In this section we highlight some opportunities that the new IT systems offer with special emphasis on enterprise resource planning systems (ERP systems). Because these systems have a common database, data only need to be stored once. The database – which stores all significant transactions – should facilitate integrated planning and follow-up. If the systems are to function properly, all metrics and responsibilities must be clearly defined. These explanations and definitions allow organisations to follow up and evaluate performance in a transparent and consistent manner. The goal is that managers should be able to use the ERP system to follow up and evaluate the outcome of decisions instead of having to piece together information from various and sundry isolated IT systems.

In other words, the ERP system can be an active component in the management control system that supports the control model used throughout the entire organisation. The prerequisite for the effective use of such ERP systems is integrated control. At the same time, the ERP system in itself contributes to integrated control (see Hedman et al., 2009, for a basic discussion of ERP systems).

An ERP system can thus increase organisational control because the system reflects the company's strategy through the metrics used and the distribution of responsibility. Through their design and use, such systems have a large influence on decision-making. In their discussion of how ERP systems in decentralised organisations contribute to the creation of a more strategically oriented management control, Lindvall and Nilsson (2009) write:

> [...] the management control system should provide the basis for management decisions, while helping to create an organisational sense-making for many co-workers. It is important that everyone

in the company has an idea of their individual and collective contribution to the whole.

LINDVALL & NILSSON, 2009, P. 111, TRANSLATED FROM SWEDISH

The issue of how to manage coordination in organisations is closely related to the concept of control. Lindvall and Nilsson (2009) explain that ERP systems use horizontal management control logic based on the organisation's refinement processes that force a higher degree of coordination. Because the activities in the processes are interdependent, even small disruptions quickly spread throughout the production system.

In this discussion of Lindvall and Nilsson's research, we also call attention to their claim that ERP systems can make management control more proactive. If we relate this claim to our discussion on the strategic dialogue, we see that such ERP systems can provide managers and co-workers with important information that is useful in their work with strategies. Finally, Lindvall and Nilsson argue that ERP systems can manage many of the problems that Johnson and Kaplan (1987) identified – that information is often received too late, is too aggregated, and may be quite irrelevant. Because such systems are built around an integrated systems solution, they can handle large amounts of data in real time very efficiently.

Another possible effect of these ERP systems is that they give organisations the opportunity to re-evaluate their control models, including how the relationship between various control tools should be clarified. Unfortunately, such opportunities are sometimes missed.

4.7 Chapter conclusions

An organisation that has an effective control can influence the behaviour of managers and co-workers so that they are in harmony with the organisation's long-term goals and strategies. This chapter addresses the issue of how to design and use management control to support the implementation and evaluation of organisational strategies chosen. We note that control requires the organisation to identify which metrics are important relative to the planning and evaluation of its strategic decisions. In addition, the organisation must identify areas of responsibility and the people with responsibility.

We argue in this chapter that a control model that is supported by structures and processes is needed if organisational control is to be achieved. Large, complex organisations today face a huge challenge when they create control packages in which the assorted components must complement each other and support the chosen strategy. We also think that management control should not be exercised too rigidly. A certain built-in flexibility is needed that supports creativity and experimentation – especially when strategies require modifications or even fundamental changes.

It is particularly important in contemporary, decentralised organisations that strategic, tactical and operational information can be exchanged easily and quickly between senior executives and the co-workers who are lower in the organisational hierarchy. Control models that use ERP systems facilitate such strategic dialogues. This is not to say that all management control in an organisation requires – or is even covered by – a control model. Although the organisation should allow flexibility, creativity and experimentation in the design and use of its control model, it is far from obvious that every control model's metrics, decisions and responsibility encourage these approaches and attitudes.

Rather, a control model should provide stability with a focus on what is important in on-going operations. To that extent, the control model is a necessary, albeit inadequate, prerequisite of control. Even when, in given situations, there is no "best" control model, some choices are certainly better than others. That explains some of the fascination of management control: the design and use of the management control system is a craft that requires understanding, experience, competences and hard work if it is to contribute to the organisation's success.

References

Anthony, Robert N. (1965). *Planning and Control Systems: A Framework for Analysis.* Boston: Harvard University Graduate School of Business Administration.

Anthony, Robert N., Govindarajan, Vijay, Hartmann, Frank G. H., Kraus, Kalle & Nilsson, Göran (2014). *Management Control Systems.* London: McGraw-Hill.

Bergstrand, Jan & Olve, Nils-Göran (1981). *Styr bättre med bättre budget.* Malmö: Liber.

Catasús, Bino (2013). Nyckeltal – vad, varför och hur? In: Jannesson, Erik & Skoog, Matti (Eds.) *Perspektiv på ekonomistyrning.* Malmö: Liber, pp. 141–160.

DiMaggio, Paul J. & Powell, Walter W. (1983). The iron cage revisited: Institutional isomorphism and collective rationality in organizational fields. *American Sociological Review* 48(2), pp. 147–160.

Hedman, Jonas, Nilsson, Fredrik & Westelius, Alf (Eds.) (2009). *Temperaturen på affärssystem i Sverige.* Lund: Studentlitteratur.

Jannesson, Erik (2014). Driving strategic change at Saab AB: The use of new control practices. In: Jannesson, Erik, Nilsson, Fredrik & Rapp, Birger (Eds.) *Strategy, Control and Competitive Advantage: Case Study Evidence.* Berlin/Heidelberg: Springer, pp. 27–57.

Jannesson, Erik, Nilsson, Fredrik & Rapp, Birger (Eds.) (2014). *Strategy, Control and Competitive Advantage: Case Study Evidence.* Berlin/Heidelberg: Springer.

Jannesson, Erik & Skoog, Matti (Eds.) (2013). *Perspektiv på ekonomistyrning.* Stockholm: Liber.

Johnsson, H. Thomas & Kaplan, Robert S. (1987). *Relevance Lost: The Rise and Fall of Management Accounting.* Boston: Harvard Business School Press.

Kaplan, Robert S. & Norton, David P. (1992). The balanced scorecard: Measures that drive performance. *Harvard Business Review* 70(1), pp. 71–79.

Kaplan, Robert S. & Norton, David P. (1996). *The Balanced Scorecard: Translating Strategy into Action.* Boston: Harvard Business School Press.

Kaplan, Robert S. & Norton, David P. (2004). *Strategy Maps: Converting Intangible Assets into Tangible Outcomes.* Boston: Harvard Business School Press.

Lindvall, Jan (2009). *Controllerns nya roll – om verksamhetsstyrning i informationsrik miljö.* Stockholm: Norstedts Akademiska Förlag.

Lindvall, Jan & Nilsson, Fredrik (2009). Från traditionell till strategisk ekonomistyrning: kan affärssystemet hantera utmaningen. In: Hedman, Jonas, Nilsson, Fredrik & Westelius, Alf (Eds.) *Temperaturen på affärssystem i Sverige.* Lund: Studentlitteratur, pp. 95–117.

Malmi, Teemu & Brown, David A. (2008). Management control systems as a package – opportunities, challenges and research directions. *Management Accounting Research* 19(4), pp. 287–300.

Nilsson, Fredrik, Olve, Nils-Göran & Parment, Anders (2011). *Controlling for Competitiveness: Strategy Formulation and Implementation through Management Control.* Malmö/Copenhagen: Liber and Copenhagen Business School Press.

Nilsson, Fredrik & Stockenstrand, Anna-Karin (2015). *Financial Accounting and Management Control: The Tensions and Conflicts Between Uniformity and Uniqueness.* Cham: Springer International Publishing Switzerland.

Olve, Nils-Göran (2014). Success through consistent strategy: How does Scania's management control matter? In: Jannesson, Erik, Nilsson, Fredrik & Rapp, Birger (Eds.) *Strategy, Control and Competitive Advantage: Case Study Evidence.* Berlin/Heidelberg: Springer, pp. 85–105.

Olve, Nils-Göran, Petri, Carl-Johan, Roy, Jan & Roy, Sofie (2003). *Making Scorecards Actionable: Balancing Strategy and Control.* Chichester: John Wiley & Sons.

Olve, Nils-Göran, Roy, Jan & Wetter, Magnus (2000). *Performance Drivers: A Practical Guide to Using the Balanced Scorecard.* Chichester: John Wiley & Sons.

Otley, David T. (1980). The contingency theory of management accounting: Achievement and prognosis. *Accounting, Organizations and Society* 5(4), pp. 413–428.

Petri, Carl-Johan & Olve, Nils-Göran (2013). Strategiorienterad styrning med hjälp av balanserade styrkort. In: Jannesson, Erik & Skoog, Matti (Eds.) *Perspektiv på ekonomistyrning.* Stockholm: Liber, pp. 161–185.

Petri, Carl-Johan & Olve, Nils-Göran (2014a). *Balanserad styrning: utveckling och tillämpning i svensk praktik.* Stockholm: Liber.

Petri, Carl-Johan & Olve, Nils-Göran (2014b). *Strategibaserad styrning: så använder du strategikartor och styrkort för att nå organisationens mål.* Stockholm: Liber.

Roberts, John (1990). Strategy and accounting in a U.K. conglomerate. *Accounting, Organizations and Society* 15(1–2), pp. 107–126.

Simons, Robert (1995). *Levers of Control: How Managers Use Innovative Control Systems to Drive Strategic Renewal.* Boston: Harvard Business School Press.

Wallander, Jan (1994). *Budgeten – ett onödigt ont.* Stockholm: SNS.

Åkesson, Johan & Siverbo, Sven (2009). Forskare varnar för överdos av styrning, *CIO Sweden,* available at [http://cio.idg.se/2.1782/1.236392/forskare-varnar-for-overdos-av-styrning] (Retrieved 26-01-2016).

5. Strategic pricing: The relationship between strategy, price models and product cost

CHRISTIAN AX, MATHIAS CÖSTER
& EINAR IVEROTH

It is often said that everything has a price. We find evidence of such a statement every day – at lunch, in a store, in the discussion of where to go on holiday. Prices often have an emotional effect. "What a bargain!" we exclaim excitedly. "It's sheer robbery!" we complain angrily. In both situations, we are reacting to prices. Our reaction is a process in which we evaluate a product price that we think reflects the reasonable (or unreasonable) value of the product[1].

Economic theory tends to explain pricing and price levels as the result of establishing equilibrium between supply and demand in a competitive market. Business theories, on the other hand, take an inside-out perspective. Therefore, a central question for a business in this context is the following: How do product prices reflect business strategy and how can they be set?

In this chapter we try to answer that question by describing models from the field of strategic management control that integrate elements of competitive strategy, customer value,

---

1 The use of the word "product" refers to both goods and services. In the digital economy it is often difficult to identify the boundary between the two. For example, mobile telephones are physical products, but they also provide services for their users.

cost structure and pricing. Our conclusion is that strategically anchored pricing is based on a certain logic (Diamantopoulos, 1991; Özer & Phillips, 2012; Olve et al., 2013). It is about making assessments and analyses of the business environment (see Chapter 3), business models and price models. But it is also necessary to use relevant costing procedures in order to arrive at a fair price level that may enable an operationalisation of price models and in the long run the business strategy.

An important starting point for this chapter is that prices are the very interface between buyers and sellers. At this interface, buyers' expectations about the value of products, and their willingness to pay for products, meet sellers' costs of producing and delivering products. Therefore, prices must include and balance both perspectives. For the seller, the price has to cover the costs of production, distribution, etc. related to the company's business strategy. There is a risk, though, that a one-sided focus on internal costs does not take into account customer values. Buyers, who rarely care about sellers' costs, are more concerned with value propositions. For example, does the smartphone customer want fast connections and the capability of synchronising work emails? Or does this customer want the capability to stream and share music with friends? Perhaps these functions are of equal importance to the customer.

Against this background, we begin the chapter by reviewing the relationships between strategies, business models and price models (for a detailed discussion of the concept of business models, see for example Baden-Fuller & Morgan, 2010; Shafer et al., 2005; Teece, 2010). The next section deals with the characteristics of price models and how, in their connection to business models, they provide a framework for a strategic discussion on how a company may charge for its products. We thereafter describe how a costing method that recognises the customer's valuation of product attributes (i.e. the characteristics or qualities that define the product from the customer perspective) can be used when a business wants to operationalise a price model. The calculation method we present is based on the Value Creation Model that McNair et al. (2001) and others have described. We conclude the chapter with a discussion on aspects of strategic pricing.

5.1 The connections between business strategy, business models and price models

A business strategy explains how a company stays competitive in the long term. Because no standard templates for business strategies exist, their design depends on, among other things, the preferred strategic approach taken (Nilsson et al., 2011). Like the business strategy, the business model is a relatively broad concept that has received increased attention quite recently (DaSilva & Trkman, 2013). The commonality among business models is their description of how a company thinks a particular business activity will contribute to its sustainable financial success.

According to Osterwalder and Pigneur (2012), a business model has nine elements, or puzzle pieces (see Figure 5.1). The main strength of their visualisation of a business model is the graphic representation of specific business logics. However, critics of this representation claim it is too linear and its underlying causal relationships are too simplistic. Most such models, however, are characterised by their simplicity.

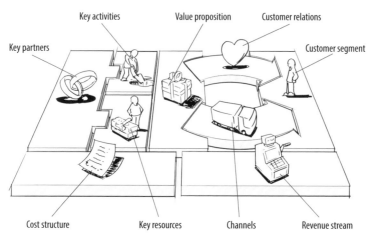

Figure 5.1 An illustration of the central elements of a business model (based on Osterwalder & Pigneur, 2012, our translation from Swedish to English).

On the left, the business model shows the elements linked to the operational cost structure. These elements are the contacts with key partners and the activities and resources needed for the creation of a product. In product costing, these elements have various essential calculation objects, such as the costs of raw materials and direct labour. The value proposition is at the centre of the business model (i.e. the value of a particular product). On the right, the business model shows the elements in the revenue stream, the customer relationships, the customer channels and the customer segments that, from a wider perspective, may also have cost implications. In other words, costs are represented in all parts of the business model although they are more explicit in certain parts than in others.

Definitions of business models are similar to those of business strategies. The difference between them, however, is mainly hierarchical. Business strategies, which take a more overarching perspective, can therefore accommodate several business models. In this perspective, the business model becomes a way to identify the decisive factors that contribute to the successful realisation of a business strategy. Olve et al. (2013) emphasise that business models are realised in various business dealings. It is at the interfaces of the business model, in the meetings between the company and its suppliers and between the company and its customers, that an understanding and an application of price models play an important role. Because price models have no generally accepted definition, in this chapter we use the definition that Olve et al. (2013, p. 11, translated from Swedish) offer:

> A price model applies to a specific business. It describes that particular arrangement: what is included, and what determines the payment.

This definition emphasises that a price model is based on a kind of understanding between buyers and sellers where there is a variety of relatively implicit agreements. Such agreements influence the relationship between buyer and seller, for example in the degree of risk sharing and of responsibility sharing. The price model, therefore, also influences how the company calculates its costs. If the company bears most of the risk, it is essential to determine how the price model influences future costs. For example, this situation may mean that certain costs should be allocated differently or even completely eliminated.

Most companies are quite capable of defining their business strategies. However, it is often rather difficult to progress from the desktop design of a product to its full realisation in a way that contributes to the company's competitiveness (Nilsson et al., 2011). In this progression, the business model and the price model are enabling concepts. Business models describe the elements behind the realisation of strategy (DaSilva & Trkman, 2013; Olve et al., 2013; Wirtz et al., 2015). The design of a price model, with its descriptions of key pricing factors, influences the realisation of the business model. It describes the key pricing factors, including how the interaction with various stakeholders in the company's environment ultimately generates revenue.

Using a metaphor for this relationship, we can say that examining a company's business activities is like examining an organism under a microscope with three lenses. At the lowest resolution, we can distinguish between the business strategy and its surroundings. When we change lenses, we see the business strategy in greater detail: the business model's customer segments and the company's key activities. With yet another lens, we can study still more details that show us what the price models, necessary for realising the business model, look like.

In the next section, as we look through the third lens, we discuss price models and how they contribute to more strategically anchored price setting.

5.2 Dimensions of price models

The digitalised society offers buyers many ways to pay for products (Dixit et al., 2008; Kung et al., 2002). As a result, many innovative price models have appeared. For example, there are situations in which customers pay what they think a product is worth. We find this price model phenomenon in many places – from some London restaurants to shareware software programmes (search for Humble Bundle on the Internet for an example) to Radiohead's alternative rock band album "In Rainbows" that, when it was released, fans could buy, download and "pay-what-you-want" for. Another price model is freemium. In this model, while the product or service is free, buyers are charged for proprietary features and other add-on products. Google, Flickr, Spotify and Gillette also use this price model.

However, there is a scarcity of research on price setting or the price models such as those just described. But, beginning in 2009, researchers have begun to show increasing interest in new and diverse perspectives on price models. For example, as shown in Figure 5.2, Olve et al. (2013) developed a meta-model pricing "equaliser" with five dimensions (see also Iveroth et al., 2013). Within the practice of price setting, as well as in the pricing literature (see for example Nagle & Hogan, 2006; Piercy et al., 2010; Macdivitt & Wilkinson, 2012) different dimensions of price models have been captured, although rarely fully. The focus is usually on defining only a single dimension, such as whether prices are set based on costs, competition or customer value.

The price model equaliser (hereafter, the equaliser) has five dimensions that together describe the basic elements of a price model. The metaphor of an equaliser is used to show that the price model should be adjusted to fit the company's view of itself in the market in the same way that the equaliser in a stereo system adjusts the audio system so that all the music played has the best sound and gives the listener the best audio experience.

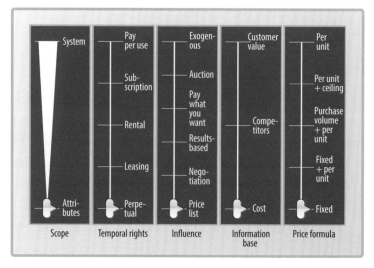

Figure 5.2 The price model equaliser and its five dimensions (based on Olve et al., 2013, our translation from Swedish to English).

Therefore, in each of the five dimensions in Figure 5.2, a control covers the various stages of the price model. Adjustment of the control settings enables analysis of how price models contribute (or do not contribute) to the realisation of a business model.

Next we describe the five dimensions in Figure 5.2. These dimensions are summarised and explained in Table 5.1, with examples of products where the particular price setting is applied.

The first dimension (Scope) concerns the scope of the offer being priced. The central issue concerns the product's core and the peripherals around that core. The dimension is shown as a sliding scale. The product system, or the package – at the top of the scale – consists of many different attributes that are priced together. Moving down the scale, the customer chooses the desired attributes. The total of the attributes the customer chooses determines the final price (e.g. the price of a Ryanair plane ticket).

The second dimension (Temporal rights) concerns the customer's rights included in a product offer. The shortest period of temporal rights is at the top of the scale when the customer pays for each use of the product. Moving down the scale, these rights increase. At the bottom of the scale, the customer has, in theory, a permanent right (including the right to resell the product).

The third dimension (Influence) highlights the balance of power between buyers and sellers in terms of pricing decisions. The key issue in this dimension is the extent of the influence of the buyer and seller on prices. At the bottom of the scale, the seller has complete control over the price list. (As an example, imagine trying to haggle over the price of a tin of tomatoes at the check-out!) Results-based pricing – mid-scale – means the price is linked to an observable outcome from the use of the product. Such pricing requires buyer and seller to agree on how results are measured. Real estate agents often use this method when establishing the selling price of apartments or houses. In exogenous pricing – at the top of the scale – neither the seller nor the buyer has power over the pricing decision because external factors completely determine the price. This type of pricing is common in long-term contracts of complex products and services. One example of such pricing is public transport in many countries. The price here is connected to a contract between a municipality and the public transport company; the price as such is linked to an index that is agreed during the price negotiations. The index formula contains various external components, such as the cost of oil, wages and GDP growth.

The fourth dimension (Information base) concerns all the information used in making pricing decisions. What do customers value? How much do competitors charge for the same products? What are the costs of development, production, distribution and sale? This is the pricing dimension that practitioners and researchers, somewhat narrowly, usually focus on.

The fifth and last dimension (Price formula) illustrates the calculations related to the prices. At the top of the scale, the customers pay for each product, and thus the total price varies with volume (or number) purchased. For example, customers may purchase petrol by the litre, or pay a lawyer by the hour. The opposite formula, at the bottom of the scale, is the fixed price. For example, a customer may pay a fixed monthly fee for a mobile phone subscription that permits unlimited usage. Several fixed and moving prices are located between these two points on the scale.

Overall, the equaliser is a tool that is useful for analysing a company's price models as well as those of its competitors. This analysis can cause a company to changes its prices and to differentiate itself from its competitors. Petri's (2014) research on price models shows that organisations often succeed with this strategy even when they make only small changes from one stage to the next within a dimension.

A contemporary example is Taxi Kurir in Sweden that charges a fixed price for taxi trips (a change from a fixed price per taxi ride to a fixed price in the Price formula dimension). Another example is car leasing. People can lease cars from most major car dealers (a change from the permanent stage to the

Table 5.1 Explanation and examples of the five dimensions in the equaliser.

Dimension	Control stage	Explanation	Example
Scope	System	A complete package of various components for a single price	All-inclusive trips
	Attributes	Each part of the offer is priced separately and the total price is based on customer choice of various attributes	Ryanair
Temporal rights	Pay per use	Payment each time the product is used	A cinema ticket
	Subscription	Regular deliveries of products not yet produced	A subscription to a daily newspaper
	Rental	An offer that is available only for a limited time period	A rented apartment
	Leasing	An offer that can be used for a limited time period with the possibility of ownership	A car lease
	Perpetual	Theoretically, the customer can use the product permanently	Clothes
Influence	Exogenous	External factors (e.g. price of oil, cost of living index, exchange rates) determine price	Public transport
	Auction	The price is determined by bidding	Ebay, Sotheby's
	Pay what you want	The buyer determines the price	Shareware, churches and cathedrals in Europe
	Results-based	The price is set based on observable results from product use	Real estate agents
	Negotiation	A discussion between seller and buyer	A bid from a carpenter
	Price list	The customer cannot negotiate because the seller has complete control over the price	Grocery stores such as Sainsbury's, Walmart

The table continues on the next page

Dimension	Control stage	Explanation	Example
Information base	Customer value	The value the customer receives	Products with strong brands such as perfumes, generic drugs
	Competitors	Competitors' price setting influences the price decision	Petrol
	Cost	Summary of costs required to develop, distribute and sell the offer	Municipal water and waste disposal
Price formula	Per unit	No ceiling because the price depends on current conditions	Petrol, cinema tickets
	Per unit + ceiling	A moving price with a ceiling	Parking fee in Stockholm, London Oyster card with capping alternative
	Purchase volume + per unit	A fixed price for a basic amount, and then payment for each new unit	Copying machine: Fixed price for the first 100 copies with an additional cost for each additional copy
	Fixed + per unit	A fixed fee combined with a price linked to the amount of consumption by the customer	Taxis, electricity
	Fixed	A fixed price regardless of the amount of customer use	Annual train ticket

leasing stage in the Rights dimension). Still another example is the cinema chain AMC in the United States. Customers can purchase a $15 ticket that allows them to watch a film as many times as they like (a change from the occasional stage to the leasing stage[2] in the Rights dimension). It is as yet unclear,

---

2 In this situation, the change may be interpreted as a change to subscription rather than to leasing. However, a subscription offers the customer a future product that has not yet been produced. In the film example, the film has been produced and can be watched during a certain timeframe.

however, how well these examples succeed as alternative price models.

If success derives from simply changing from one stage to another, why don't more companies just do that? To answer that question, we need to study price models in relation to both business models and business strategy in the relevant context. A business model can contain several different price models that (hopefully) interact. When a price model is changed, it is necessary to analyse the effect on other price models as well as on the business model. Such analysis should take into consideration the value proposition, the key factors that generate revenues and incur costs, and the possibilities and obstructions related to different price models. Successfully designing price models that support the business model is an important step on the way to achieving profitable and sustainable competitive advantage.

5.2.1 StayTheNight – a price model example

To illustrate how price models can be analysed and developed, we use examples from the hotel industry.[3] Here we describe the aspects that relate to revenues in business models – hence, a price model that interfaces with the customers.

StayTheNight is a hotel chain that has a business model in which the value proposition consists of affordable and

---

3 The example is based on research conducted at the School of Business, Economics and Law at the University of Gothenburg. We use this fictitious name for an actual hotel chain. The example has no connection with the Stay the Night B&B in New York City. In the pricing examples, we use our own analysis of the possible options presented.

quiet nights in central city locations. The idea is that every hotel in the chain should be no more than 10 minutes' walk to the central train station or other travel centre. Customers are mainly business people who need a hotel room for only one or two nights. Rooms are simple but fairly spacious and in good condition. The hotel chain's price model (see Figure 5.3) is as follows: The Scope is "System" (the room price includes breakfast, Wi-Fi, etc.); the Temporal Rights are "Pay per use"; the Influence is "Price list"; the Information base is "Competitors"; and the Price formula is "Per unit" (the hotel guests pay per night).

In the hotel industry, owing to various digital search services, prices are reasonably transparent. Customers can easily compare various hotels' amenities, locations and, most

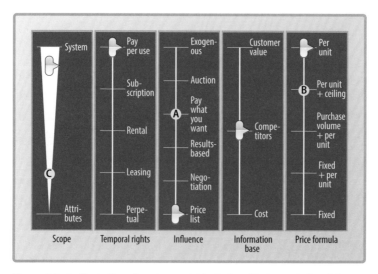

Figure 5.3 An illustration of a price model in the hotel industry. A, B and C are examples of possible changes to the model (based on Olve et al., 2013, our translation from Swedish to English).

importantly, prices when making reservations. StayTheNight, which promotes affordability as part of its value proposition, is well aware of the importance of pricing. For example, should StaytheNight try to compete with lower prices? The risk of this strategy – assuming the same number of guests – is that revenue will be less, making it more difficult to cover fixed costs. It is also a challenge to have to spend time monitoring competitors' prices when a low-price strategy is adopted. If such short-term decisions are taken, there may also be negative repercussions for the overall implementation of business strategy. Instead of focusing on price levels, StayTheNight may have a better chance of gaining competitive advantage by changing its price model.

So how can a business change its price model? Figure 5.3 presents three options: A, B and C. It is possible to make changes in more than one dimension. However, as we noted in the previous section, research shows that when price model changes occur, they are often made in a single dimension.

Option A allows hotel guests to pay the amount they wish to pay instead of a sum from the price list. This is a rather radical option, however, that one is unlikely to find in the hotel industry. While Option A would very likely increase customer flow, total revenues would likely decline. Option A poses considerable risk for the hotel chain. Without any knowledge of how much the customers will pay, StayTheNight cannot estimate its cash flow. The risk could perhaps be somewhat reduced if the "what-you-want" price offer were combined with some kind of floor (i.e. a minimum price required). Nevertheless, this price model is consistent with the hotel chain's claim that a night's stay should be reasonably priced.

Option B encourages hotel guests to make repeat reservations. The guests pay a certain ceiling amount that gives them free stays for a particular period of time, possibly for the current year. This price model will probably appeal to the hotel chain's main customer segment – business travellers. For such customers, the hotel chain may be their first choice, and thereby StayTheNight may be able to realise its business model. Of course, other hotels also have customer bonus programmes that offer free stays. The difference with Option B, however, is that the bonus is rewarded more directly and may include several free stays in a certain time period.

A problem arises with Option B, however, in deciding on the ceiling amount and the number of free stays. How many stays are reasonable: 10 or 20 nights? Maybe 30 nights? And should the offer apply only for stays paid by the company? The price model also means quite a high degree of risk for StayTheNight. If the ceiling is too low, revenue is lost while fixed hotel costs remain constant. Or, if the ceiling is too high, customers will turn away. Thus, StayTheNight has the challenge of calculating the number of additional hotel stays up to the ceiling and the number of hotel stays after the ceiling is reached. Maybe the two will cancel each other out?

Option C links the value proposition to the idea of affordability. Although affordability is not the same as low-cost, it is still an important price model description because it indicates that a particular company may have lower prices than those of its competitors. For example, when Ryanair entered the deregulated European aviation market, the company promoted its low prices. Some flight tickets sold by established airlines, which included many attributes, lay in the upper part of the Scope dimension while Ryanair divided its value proposition so that the Scope dimension became an "attribute". The advertised Ryanair price was only for a seat on the plane; customers had to pay for all other attributes (e.g. luggage handling, food, check-in etc.). Although promoted as a low-cost airline, once customers realised they had to pay Ryanair for these various attributes that other airlines included in the price of a ticket, they saw that the price difference was not as much as they first thought.

For StayTheNight, this price model allows it to compete on the basis of price. However, a disadvantage is the loss of customer patronage and loyalty if customers feel they have been tricked. When it comes to Ryanair, many customers have criticised the company for exactly this reason, but the company nevertheless maintains high turnover and achieves very satisfactory profits.[4]

These three price models exemplify how companies can change their price models when they operate in markets where price transparency prevails and the competition is significant. Changing a price model is an important step toward implementing strategies and realising business models. To make these changes fully operational, companies must then make the necessary calculations that support their pricing decisions. In the next section we describe how to make such calculations.

5.3 Pricing, customer value and cost structure

Regardless of the price model it uses, a company's revenues must, in the long term, exceed its costs in order to achieve

---

4 Between 2011 and 2014, Ryanair increased turnover by about 39% and profit by about 35% (Ryanair, 2015).

a satisfactory return.[5] Traditional product costing that uses cost items – for example, direct labour, direct materials and overhead costs – is not supportive of business strategy. This is because the value of a product is defined by the customer, not by the cost. For this reason, traditional costing methods should be re-examined and revised in the strategic context.

Newer approaches to strategic management control (e.g. McNair-Connolly et al., 2013) typically adopt a customer perspective on value. In one development, product attributes (i.e. qualities or characteristics that define a product from the customer perspective) are in focus. All products have a set of value attributes. When customers have a choice of products, their purchase decisions are not random. On the contrary, because customers usually have a rather good idea of what they want to buy, they examine the value proposition of the different choices in order to judge their value. They make their final purchase selection based on their evaluations of the products' value attributes.

The key value attributes in the automotive sector, for example, include safety, reliability, power and image. In the restaurant sector, the key value attributes are the menu, location, service and (perhaps) trendiness. The equaliser, with its five dimensions, shows that the Scope dimension is a system with a sliding scale divided into various value attributes.

From this perspective, the value of a product – its value proposition, i.e. the value of all the attributes embedded in a product – is determined by the customer. Thus, value propositions are the basis for customers making choices among

---

5 This section is based on Ax et al., 2015.

competing products. This perspective also means that the customers' evaluations of product attributes are weakly related to the companies' costs of providing the attributes. Therefore, customer value and product cost need not positively relate to each other. For example, higher customer value does not necessarily mean companies will incur higher product attribute costs (or vice versa). Nor does this perspective mean that companies should aim for the lowest cost for delivering product attributes. For example, restaurants' value propositions are the same: food, service and location. Yet the qualities of these attributes may vary greatly.

Companies therefore must align consumer preferences and resource consumption – an idea that is consistent with the business model and the price model. The configuration of the price model influences customer behaviour. In the dimension of Price formula in the equaliser (see Figure 5.2), a product can have a fixed price, a per unit price, or some combination of the two. If the price is fixed (e.g. a fixed price of 299 crowns per month for a mobile phone, with unlimited internet access), the customer is likely to use the product more than if the price were variable (e.g. 1 crown per MB of surfing with monthly billing). If the marginal cost of an additional unit of resource consumption is low (e.g. as in digital services), there are no significant additional costs. Given this perspective, the fixed cost alternative may create a competitive advantage. On the other hand, if the resource consumption is more evident (for example, each hotel room rental means additional resource consumption from the activities of cleaning and linen/towel changes), a per unit price may be the better alternative.

The Value Creation Model (VCM) attempts to align

customer preferences and resource consumption (McNair, 1994; McNair et al., 2001; McNair-Connelly et al., 2013). More specifically, the VCM attempts to match customers' valuation of product attributes (i.e. willingness to pay) and a company's activity costs for providing these attributes. The VCM reflects the key elements of the business model (see Figure 5.1). The company's activity costs are on the left side of the figure, the company's value proposition (i.e. a product or value attributes) is in the middle of the figure, and the customer's valuation perspective on product attributes is on the right side of the figure.

In practical situations, the VCM attempts to do more than just match consumer preferences and spending. The VCM also has a number of analytical features that focus on the relationship between price, cost and value attributes. We next highlight the central features of the model.

5.3.1 StayTheNight – an illustrative example

There are different approaches for determining the customer value of a product. One approach assumes that the willingness to pay for a product is a relevant indication of customer value, particularly when product prices are determined by the market (i.e. when the individual firm has no influence over prices). The price a product commands in the market is a signal of its perceived customer value, and thus indicates the economic value that customers derive from the bundle of attributes embedded in the product. To assess customers' willingness to pay for a product, information on which value attributes

Table 5.2 Guest valuation of product attributes at StayTheNight.

Product attribute	Customer value (%)	Customer value (SEK)
Breakfast	23	276
Room cleaning	20	240
Welcome	17	204
Food/drink in the restaurant	15	180
Room furnishings	10	120
Bathroom amenities	10	120
Internet access	5	60
Total	100	1,200

customers value and the relative importance of each attribute in the buying decisions are needed.

The hotel chain StayTheNight offers customers seven main product attributes (see Table 5.2; monetary amounts are in Swedish crowns: SEK). Randomly selected customers were asked to divide 100 points (converted to percentages) among the seven attributes based on their willingness to pay for the attributes. The price of the room (SEK 1,200) was then allocated to the attributes on the basis of these percentages.

The calculated values, also called revenue equivalents, indicate, on average, how much the hotel customers are willing to pay for the value attributes (i.e. the amount of hotel revenues that can be attributed to each value attribute). To a considerable extent, customer value varies with the hotel category and with the customers themselves. Because StayTheNight belongs to a large hotel chain in which customers are primarily business people, customer value should take this market niche into account.

In the next step, activities related to the product attributes are identified and costed. Table 5.3 presents the calculation, on an annual basis, of StaytheNight's activity costs per product attribute for an overnight stay (see below for an explanation of each cost category). Note that Table 5.3 includes only costs related to the product attributes, and does not include other indirect hotel costs.

If we compare Table 5.2 and Table 5.3, we conclude that customer value (see Table 5.2, column "Customer value"), exceeds the total cost of each product attribute. Although this is important information, from a customer strategic perspective, it is more interesting to compare the customer value with the activity costs that create customer value.

The total product attribute costs in the first column of Table 5.3 are split into three cost categories. *Value add costs* are

Table 5.3 Costs (in SEK) for the product attributes that are included in one night's stay at StayTheNight. The calculation is the sum of the activity costs per product attribute/number of guests = total cost per product attribute.

Product attribute	Total costs	Value add costs	Support costs	Waste costs
Breakfast	90	60	22	8
Room cleaning	100	75	20	5
Welcome	80	45	31	4
Food/drink in the restaurant	95	40	25	30
Room furnishings	30	20	5	5
Bathroom amenities	40	25	11	4
Internet access	4	4	0	0
Total	439	269	114	56

the share of the activity costs that add customer value to the product attribute and that generate revenue.

Support costs, or business value-add activity costs, are the share of the total activity costs that do not contribute to customer value but are necessary for many business operations in both the short and the long term.

Support costs may include costs related to activities such as billing, reservations, administration, product development and accounting. Certain support costs are referred to as hygiene costs (or activities) because they are an integral and natural part of business relationships (e.g. billing, transportation and returns management). Competent performance of these activities does not cause the customer to place a higher value on a purchase or a service. However, poor performance can negatively influence the customer's perception of that purchase or service.

Waste costs are the share of the total activity costs that neither increase customer value nor facilitate a business entity's operations. Inefficiency, bureaucracy and unnecessary work are examples of waste costs.

Overall, because support costs and waste costs do not contribute to customer value, they do not contribute to revenue generation. Thus, all amounts spent on support costs and waste costs reduce earnings. Put more dramatically, such costs come out of profit without increasing customer value. This means that the company could improve its profitability without affecting customer value if it could reduce these costs.

A key purpose of the VCM is to develop and analyse value multipliers. A value multiplier is calculated by relating customer value in financial terms to the value add cost of each attribute associated with a particular product. Each attribute thus has its own multiplier that indicates how much revenue each Swedish crown earns. In other words, a value multiplier measures the degree of alignment between a value attribute's revenue equivalent – the amount customers are willing to pay for the value attribute – and the cost of the customer value-adding activity.

Table 5.4 presents the value multipliers for StayTheNight. The hotel chain's guests provide the information on customer satisfaction with the attributes in terms of their willingness to pay for the attributes. Table 5.2 and Table 5.3 provide the data for the analysis. For example, the value multiplier for the product attribute "Breakfast" is calculated as Customer value / Value costs = 276/60 = 4.6.

As Table 5.4 shows, revenues from each StayTheNight's product attribute exceed its cost. For example, each Swedish crown spent on Breakfast results in revenue of 4.6 crowns, and each crown spent on Welcome results in revenue of 4.53 crowns.

Table 5.4 Value multipliers for customer satisfaction with product attributes at StayTheNight.

Product attribute	Value multiplier	Customer satisfaction (%)
Breakfast	4.6	84
Room cleaning	3.2	92
Welcome	4.53	92
Food/drink in the restaurant	4.5	84
Room furnishings	6	86
Bathroom amenities	4.8	78
Internet access	15	98

5.3.2 Use of the Value Creation Model

A value multiplier, at its lowest, can have a zero value, which means that customers are unwilling to pay any amount for an attribute, and may in principle assume any amount of value. In practice, however, price restrictions limit the size. To simplify this idea, let us assume that a value multiplier can be described as high or low relative to other value multipliers or in comparison with the average value of a company's value multipliers.

Low value multipliers, particularly those lower than the average of a company's value multipliers, suggest that the company uses too many activity resources on its value attributes. There are several explanations for low value multipliers. For example, customers may be reluctant to pay for an attribute because they think the value attribute is of low quality, or inefficiencies exist in the performance of activities, or the company is at a cost disadvantage because of its limited ability to differentiate its products and their value attributes. The company can take various measures to increase its value multipliers by reducing its resource consumption, by streamlining its production of value attributes, or by differentiating its products or value attributes. These actions may increase current customers' willingness to pay as well as attract new customers.

While the interpretation of low value multipliers indicates that the company probably uses too many resources on the creation of its value attributes, the interpretation of high value multipliers requires information about customer satisfaction with the value attributes. There are two basic explanations why a higher degree of alignment between activity costs and value attributes contributes to a higher degree of customer satisfaction and, ultimately, to a higher degree of customer loyalty – both of which have a positive influence on the company's financial performance.

When a value multiplier is high and customer satisfaction is low, this indicates that the company is not spending enough on its value attribute. As a result, revenue and costs related to the value attribute are not aligned.

However, if the value multiplier is high and customer satisfaction is also high, it signals that the company has a competitive advantage. This means that customers are willing to pay a fairly high amount for a value attribute that does not cost the company a great deal. In such situations, a company can exploit its competitive advantage, for example, by increasing its price (assuming the market permits), by raising the market profile of its products through "playing up" its competitive advantage in marketing programmes, by offering greater customer value at a lower cost (resulting in increased profit), or by reducing its activity costs (resulting in lower sales prices and unchanged or increased profit).

Table 5.4 also presents the customer satisfaction percentages for StayTheNight's various attributes. The customer degree of satisfaction varies from a low of 78% to a high of 98%. The percentage for "Internet access" (98%) indicates that the hotel chain has a competitive advantage with this attribute even though the "Customer value" for "Internet access" is only 5% (see Table 5.2). Overall customer satisfaction reveals high values except for the attribute of "Bathroom amenities" (78%). StayTheNight may want to promote its "Internet access" attribute and investigate the low satisfaction with "Bathroom amenities".

Close analysis of value multipliers can provide a company

with useful information in several contexts. Price setting can be adapted to the size of the value multipliers. For example, high value multipliers indicate that prices may be raised. A company may also use its value multipliers to divide its customers into product segments on the basis of distinct value profiles. Also a company's marketing programmes and sales efforts can be adapted to various value profiles. Further, the VCM's categorisation of costs can be the basis of various specific actions.

Another less tangible, but no less significant, potential advantage of value multipliers is that they can raise awareness of a company's opportunities and threats, reveal new insights about the product attributes, and promote dialogue across organisational functional boundaries. As a result, issues related to the company's customer perspective, its products and its cost structure are addressed.

The VCM is a model that takes into account key elements in the company's business model. It differs from traditional calculation models in that it includes the company's customers in a way that makes their preferences the starting point for the internal analysis. Through a comprehensive analysis, the VCM focuses on customer valuation (i.e. the customer's willingness to pay) of product attributes, the company's activity costs for its product attributes, and the company's value proposition. All these data stemming from the VCM are valuable when developing price models and business models.

5.4 Chapter conclusions

In this chapter we examined how an organisation can implement and develop its business strategy using strategically anchored pricing. From the perspective that strategy is something we design, price is an output that enables us to realise our strategy. Strategy thus becomes the basis of our business model design, in particular with reference to how we formulate our value proposition. The price model will then function as an interface between our customers and the organisation that communicates the value proposition. Our price model – how we set prices for our products – should therefore reflect and extend our strategy. Whether or not the price model is a successful extension of the strategy depends on how well goals for turnover, profit, market share and so forth are achieved.

If we instead consider business strategy as something that essentially emerges from existing business activities, then price models have a somewhat different role. Because price models are at the interface of relationships with our customers, a change in those relationships means that our price model must also change. The way our price model changes will then influence our business model. For example, do we need to examine the channels to our customers in order to reformulate our value proposition? Following such an analysis, we may find that we should adjust or even change our strategy. In this way, strategy evolves. If our price model proves sufficiently successful, other actors (i.e. competitors) may react by changing their price models. These changes will in turn influence other price models. Then we may have to review our price model and our business model, and so on.

Finally, we refer to the question we asked in the introduction to this chapter: How do product prices reflect business strategy and how can they be set? In answering this question, we promoted strategically anchored pricing that has a logical basis. This requires analysing and evaluating a company's business environment as well as its business model and price-model. Calculations are needed in order to set reasonable price levels consistent with the company's price model and, ultimately, with its business strategy.

In the chapter we have described two methods of strategic management control: price model analysis and customer value-based calculation that, when correctly applied, help to link price setting with issues of competitive strategy. By extension, this means that price setting has a substantial influence on strategic management control. Using our price models, we must ensure that our management control models contribute to the realisation of our strategy, business models and price models. In short, as the examples in this chapter show, price setting is a strategic management control issue.

References

Ax, Christian, Johansson, Christer & Kullvén, Håkan (2015). *Den nya ekonomistyrningen*. Stockholm: Liber.

Baden-Fuller, Charles & Morgan, Mary S. (2010). Business models as models. *Long Range Planning* 43(2–3), pp. 156–171.

DaSilva, Carlos M. & Trkman, Peter (2013). Business model: What it is and what it is not. *Long Range Planning* 47(6), pp. 379–389.

Diamantopoulos, Adamantios (1991). Pricing: theory and evidence – a literature review. In: Baker, Michael J. (Ed.), *Perspectives on Marketing Management*. London: John Wiley & Sons, pp. 63–192.

Dixit, Ashutosh, Whipple, Thomas W., Zinkhan, Georg M. & Gailey, Edward (2008). A taxonomy of information technology-enhanced pricing strategies. *Journal of Business Research* 61(4), pp. 275–283.

Iveroth, Einar, Westelius, Alf, Petri, Carl-Johan, Olve, Nils-Göran, Cöster, Mathias & Nilsson, Fredrik (2013). How to differentiate by price: Proposal for a five-dimensional model. *European Management Journal* 31(2), pp. 109–123.

Kung, Mui, Monroe, Kent B. & Cox, Jennifer L. (2002) Pricing on the Internet. *Journal of Product & Brand Management* 11(5), pp. 274–288.

Macdivitt, Harry & Wilkinson, Mike (2012). *Value-Based Pricing: Drive Sales and Boost Your Bottom Line by Creating, Communicating and Capturing Customer Value.* New York: McGraw Hill.

McNair, Carol J. (1994). *The Profit Potential – Taking High Performance to the Bottom Line.* Hoboken: John Wiley & Sons.

McNair Carol J., Politnik, Lidija & Silvi, Riccardo (2001). Cost management and value creation: The missing link. *European Accounting Review* 10(1), pp. 33–50.

McNair-Connolly, Carol J., Polutnik, Lidija, Silvi, Riccardo & Watts, Ted (2013). *Value Creation in Management Accounting – Using Information to Capture Customer Value.* New York: Business Expert Press.

Nagle, Thomas T. & Hogan, John E. (2006). *The Strategy and Tactics of Pricing: A Guide to Growing More Profitably.* Upper Saddle River: Pearson/Prentice Hall.

Nilsson, Fredrik, Olve, Nils-Göran, & Parment, Anders (2011). *Controlling for Competitiveness: Strategy Formulation and Implementation through Management Control.* Malmö: Liber and Copenhagen: Copenhagen Busines School Press.

Olve, Nils-Göran, Cöster, Mathias, Iveroth, Einar, Petri, Carl-Johan & Westelius, Alf (2013). *Prissättning: Affärsekologier, affärsmodeller, prismodeller.* Lund: Studentlitteratur.

Osterwalder, Alexander & Pigneur, Yves (2012). *Business Model Generation: en handbok för visionärer, banbrytare och utmanare.* Lund: Studentlitteratur.

Petri, Carl-Johan (2014). Using an innovative price model to leverage the business model – The case of price model innovation in the largest Swedish taxi company. *Journal of Business Models* 2(1), pp. 56–70.

Piercy, Nigel, Cravens, David & Lane, Nikala (2010). Thinking strategically about pricing decisions. *Journal of Business Strategy* 31(5), pp. 38–48.

Ryanair (2015). Statement. [http://corporate.ryanair.com/investors/statement/] (Retrieved 03-02-2015).

Shafer, Scott M., Smith, H. Jeff & Linder, Jane C. (2005). The power of business models. *Business Horizons* 48(3), pp. 199–207.

Teece, David J. (2010). Business models, business strategy and innovation. *Long Range Planning* 43(2–3), pp. 172–194.

Wirtz, Bernd W., Pistoia, Adriano, Ullrich, Sebastian, Göttel, Vincent (2015). Business models: Origin, development and future research. *Long Range Planning* 49(1), pp. 36–54.

Özer, Özalp & Phillips, Robert (2012). *The Oxford Handbook of Pricing Management.* Oxford: Oxford University Press.

6. Controlling and being controlled

BINO CATASÚS & MIKAEL CÄKER

A fundamental question in the management control literature is: "How can you motivate people to do something they may not want to do?" Depending on how we choose to answer this question, we will have different views on how technological market conditions influence our organisations and the opportunities and limitations in acquiring intellectual and material resources. Our perceptions of co-workers – how they relate to their workplace and how they are motivated – will influence our answer. What might at first seem to be a simple question is less so when we consider today's complex workplace conditions.

In addressing this generic control question with commentary on societal changes, some authors advocate control that does not retreat from complexity. Is it possible that people want only some of the things the organisation wants because the organisation wants so many things? Does the organisation want something that, to a substantial degree, can be developed in dialogue with its various parts? Is it not rather difficult to distinguish between the organisation and its co-workers? If the answer to all these questions is "yes", it seems reasonable that the discussion should broaden from how to monitor co-workers to a focus on facilitating work and formulating goals and strategies.

As early as the mid-1970s, Olve (1977) analysed "multi-objective planning dialogue" in his doctoral dissertation (see also Chapter 2). This pioneering choice of the words "multiobjective" and "dialogue" broke with the tradition that viewed successful management control as strongly linked to the formulation of financial goals and to the efficient, top-down flow of information in the organisational hierarchy. The idea that management control deals with multiple objectives appeared prominently in the debate in the 1990s after Kaplan and Norton (1996) published their bestselling book on the balanced scorecard. The research by Olve and his colleagues (Olve et al., 1997) on the same theme has now spread to many parts of the globe.

A clear difference between the Swedish and the American research is apparent in the discussion of how the balanced scorecard is produced and used. This difference relates specifically to the dialogue with, and the role of, the people who are controlled (hereafter, the controlled) (Johanson et al., 2001; Ax & Bjørnenak, 2005). The Swedish view in the discussion is that even when the organisation has developed a "balanced" approach to defining its objectives, this approach is insufficient. Instead, because organisations are difficult to control, they should always maintain flexibility, given that most organisations must constantly adapt to their changing environments (see Chapter 4). Successful control depends on knowing where important information can be found, and on how co-workers can participate in the control process (Olve, 1977).

However, the consequences of multiobjective control may be negative as well as positive (Cäker, 2007). The inherent problem of multiobjective control is that, inevitably, objectives may conflict. In such situations, other organisational control mechanisms (such as bonuses and responsibility delegation) motivate people to use numbers as "ammunition" (Burchell et al., 1980). Such conflicts may be partly resolved if other processes are available in which the controlled can become involved in control issues in meaningful ways, for example by participating in the dialogue on key figures, planning and monitoring.

In this chapter we discuss and analyse the strong focus on *dialogue* in the management control literature of the early twenty-first century. This literature emphasises how the controlled play a central role in organisations and how a space is created for them in the formal control system. Our comments link to the discussion on control in Chapter 2 that treats the importance of narratives in which the controlled can take an active role.

The chapter begins with a description of how the management control literature increasingly focuses on the use of control in relation to its design. This focus allows us to examine the role of dialogue. Next, we discuss why the need for dialogue has increased. Outside pressure (e.g. government regulations and mass media interest) to increase control creates the risk that the design of control can take several directions and increases the need for dialogue. We conclude the chapter with a discussion on how organisations can create conditions in which the controlled see control as enabling.

6.1 The use of control and the voice of the controlled

Control is often divided between the design of the control measures and the use of the control measures. Traditionally, management control has focused on design, from both a theoretical and a practical perspective. Its underlying logic is that control sends certain signals to co-workers that cause them to react appropriately. This logic means that questions relating to the use of control are perceived as relatively unproblematic (see Figure 6.1).

This control model assumes that senior managers, after they have decided on the objectives of the organisation's activities, will choose a control design that supports those objectives. The most common way of preparing a control design is to start with ideas from agency theory that claim that controls and incentives are the methods (as well as the agency costs incurred) principals will use when trying to align interests (Jensen & Meckling, 1976). These agency costs can reduce or even prevent opportunistic behaviour. In principle, agency theory suggests that (i) when the controls are designed to reward higher production rates, co-workers will focus on production improvements and (ii) when senior managers establish control measures for areas of responsibility, accountability will steer the organisation toward its objectives.

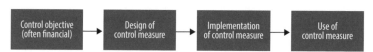

Figure 6.1 Traditional control logic.

Olve (1977) criticises this linear (and obviously simplified) idea concerning the possibilities of control. He explains that the organisation in practice has multiple objectives and that the success of control depends on on-going discussions (i.e. dialogues) around its objectives, design, implementation and use. This focus on dialogue is a way to emphasise that control is unlikely to succeed if a mechanistic model, such as that shown in Figure 6.1, drives development. If the organisation is to learn how best to achieve its overall objectives, it is essential to listen to the controlled regarding their perceptions of their work situation. This, in turn, has important implications when choosing the most reasonable control objectives and measures.

In the research literature, the discussion by Simons (e.g. 1995) on the "levers of control" focused attention on the use of management control.[1] Simons suggests that there are four different dimensions of use that are vital for successful strategy implementation and development. Beliefs systems and boundary systems (the first two controls) must be clearly defined. These controls form the outer framework of control that co-workers must relate to. The third control system is diagnostic control by which top managers create a flow of information that allows them to track the development and performance of the organisation's activities. In addition, such information facilitates the traditional control of co-workers using monitoring, following-up and rewards.

The literature has focused mainly on Simons' fourth control system – interactive control. This control is intended to ensure that senior managers participate in on-going communications

---

1 The "levers of control" (Simons, 1995) are further explained in Chapter 4.

related to strategic uncertainties and other important areas. The controlled have useful information on the activities they work with. According to Simons (1995), the organisation must ensure that such information reaches top management. The role of the controlled in interactive control is thus more active than in traditional control models. They can influence the organisation by their experience, and not just by their performance.

Simons (1995) claims that senior managers must determine which organisational areas are central and therefore require interactive control. However, other researchers have developed the concept more generally so that interactive control also refers to the organisation's ability to help co-workers provide key information to top management. Neither Simons nor Olve claims that dialogue is important in itself; rather, the function of dialogue is to draw attention to the constant need for the development of strategy and to the influence of operations on strategy. The concept of interactive control has thus strengthened the role of the controlled in the management control literature.

Frow et al. (2010) offered a notable contribution to the "levers of control" discussion in their article on budgetary control. In a case study of a multinational technology company in a rapidly-changing industry, these authors developed the concept of "continuous budgeting". They emphasise that a highly traditional budgeting process can play a significant role – even in complex and dynamic activities – if the structures for making changes are orderly. The logic is that the people (the controlled) with budgetary responsibility have the right to request support for the company's objectives; if the support is insufficient, they have the right to request that these objectives be reviewed. The controlled should have a voice in deciding when it is necessary to review objectives.

Frow et al. (2010) describe how the organisation's incentive system is based on the idea that the best performance is to achieve budget targets. However, quick responses and clear communications about the risk of missed budget targets are also acceptable. What is not acceptable is the failure to mention the problem and then report that budget targets have not been met. The control mix in the organisation provides the support tools for the processes that can change and anchor budgetary goals. Formal structures exist to ensure that the controlled in the organisation have the opportunity to be heard.

While the article by Frow et al. (2010) does not respond to all the issues related to the much criticised traditional budget (see Wallander, 1999), it is interesting in that it focuses our attention on the on-going use of, and potential change in, budgets, and on how budgets are both interactive and diagnostic control tools. In their case, budgets are diagnostic until middle managers argue that they should be interactive. Importantly, however, this metamorphosis of the budget requires on-going dialogues with the parties involved.

Frow et al. (2010) also show the role of boundary and beliefs control systems in enabling budgetary targets to be taken seriously. The idea is that it is better to signal an organisation's inability to achieve its goals than to ignore the problem and then report missed budgetary goals. Management's ability to clarify this order of priorities is important for achieving a balance between budgeted goals and commitments and the possibility of adjusting them when necessary.

The "levers of control" literature has helped promote the

idea that the controlled play an active role in organisations, and that dialogue is a part of control activities. In the next section we argue that such dialogues should be increased because of the greater complexity of many operations and the greater demands on co-workers and the organisation for internal and external efficiency. As a result, extensive organisational review and reporting – with greater attention paid to monitoring and balancing the people who work with the operational activities – have increased.

6.2 The role of accounting and the risk of overdose

The role of accounting in management control has been a major issue since the 1980s. Some researchers have questioned whether accounting can contribute to management control given that it produces information in a relatively rigid format, with a strong financial emphasis (Kaplan & Johnson, 1987; Olve et al., 1997). The assumed problem of trying to control operations with a one-dimensional and frequently naive description of operations has been turned into an argument about the increasing importance of non-financial disclosures. It should be emphasised that the movement from a one-dimensional management control model to a multiobjective control model (that includes non-financial measurements) does not challenge the idea that a company's ultimate goal is to succeed financially. The argument is that including non-financial measurements of operations is useful in implementing strategies and in identifying relationships between operations and profitability.

At the same time that multiobjective control has become

more and more accepted, organisational leaders find that the surrounding society and increasingly complex operations drive a need to deal with still more aspects of control. This development is especially evident as more areas and activities (personnel, product quality, the environment, security, key accounts, cash flow and so on) are viewed as strategically important. As a result, the concept of control has expanded. This has occurred in conjunction with the advances in IT systems that create greater opportunities – at no significant increase in direct costs – to store data, to access plans, and to monitor detailed activities remotely, even from distant locations.

Furthermore, as the market for control instruments has expanded, many consulting firms and systems vendors now spend considerable time and resources trying to convince decision-makers that they need to develop (i.e. intensify) their control. Still another development is that the focus on corporate governance and financial accounting issues has greatly increased. For example, recent legislation related to financial accounting reporting, conflicts of interest and policies requires more disclosure by public companies of detailed information as well as reports on how control is exercised (i.e. risk management). Governments have also demanded more disclosures from public institutions and from not-for-profit entities. In short, all these developments have caused companies and other organisations to examine and improve their control systems and to disclose more information on these systems.

Some people in organisations, especially the controlled, find this increased focus on control does not necessarily support them in their work. Accounting information and disclosure reports, broadly speaking, sometimes send conflicting signals to co-workers about what is important. The risk is that co-workers may be confused by this overdose of control. For example, governments may issue detailed instructions to retirement home staff on how to protect the elderly and guarantee them a minimum level of service. However, these instructions may conflict with the staff's professional opinions and management's ideas (and even with the views of the elderly themselves) on how services should be provided. Although the existence of conflicting objectives is not new, the new control systems that require certain actions and procedures make these conflicts more obvious.

Moreover, with the demand for greater control, more information on control systems must be developed, produced and communicated. As a result, the administration of control systems increases greatly. When managers, whatever their level, have more administrative tasks ("paperwork"), they have less time for operations. Too often, this overdose of control also means that the controlled are required to prioritise various activities – a task they are not trained or educated to perform. Even more serious, too much control may cause people in an organisation to set aside their own experience and judgement as they obediently follow the control procedures and demands without protest or challenge (Catasús & Grönlund, 2005).

Such situations, which create both an organisational problem and a human problem, are worrisome. For the organisation, this means that managers at various levels are required to choose among the different objectives. Compliance with strategy may be damaged if they choose differently.[2] For the co-workers, a range of objectives may cause workplace stress, illness and demotivation. The Swedish Social Insurance Agency (Försäkringskassan, 2015) reports that stress-related illnesses have generally increased among people at work. This stress is often caused by the imbalance between work demands and work resources when control is a main mediator between the organisation and the people it employs.

Messner (2009) discusses the potential problems when organisations offer co-workers multiple ways to report on their performance. Although this development may increase the opportunity for co-workers to make their performance visible, Messner (Ibid.) claimed that more reporting channels lead to more reporting demands. Ultimately, co-workers find this complex situation unsustainable. Cäker (2007) describes such a situation in which an increased focus on non-financial key figures related to customer focus seemed unreasonable when set against the requirements related to financial performance. Messner (2009) suggests that "self-management" is a risky idea if managers promote the idea without considering that co-workers need reasonable tasks they can manage.

The controlled may think multiobjective control is somewhat of an overdose of control. However, the logic of such control is often irrefutable. Most people agree that short and long-term organisational perspectives, shareholder and societal benefit, strict quality processes, flexible customer solutions, and internal and external efficiency are all important parts of

---

2 From a management perspective, compliance with strategy is desirable. However, even poor compliance can, over time, lead to strategic development – a positive organisational result.

today's demands. Still, because these objectives may be contra-dictory, a time may come when the co-worker has to choose between, say, a long-term and a short-term goal. In fact, Lillis' (2002) study suggests that there is an inherent contradiction between a customer focus and an efficiency focus when specific dimensions of performance are addressed. Thus, the controlled are hesitant regarding the effects of multidimensional control. While they accept many objectives should be considered, they also suspect some objectives may be contradictory.

Michael Power's book, *The Audit Society* (1999), significantly influenced the accounting literature and has, arguably, also affected accounting practice. Although the book deals with the increase of auditing activities (financial and non-financial) all through society, Power's narrative parallels the rise of organi-sational control in its various aspects. The motivation for the increase in control (and in audits) can be understood as an increased belief in agency theory and in the idea that activi-ties on all levels should be controlled. Control models exist for seemingly everything – from quality issues to sustainability issues. Control is no longer a matter for a few experts; control is an issue for every member of the organisation. Control, as an ideal, is not delimited to a particular time and place. Rather, control is found in every practice. Thus, the control technolo-gies have become obligatory parts of the organisational design at all levels. Further, as the members of organisations are, in some ways, more influential for innovation and performance, the co-workers and the managers are increasingly involved in control activities. In fact, more people in organisations have a dual role: they control and they are controlled. It can be argued that, today, control is an issue of concern even at the lowest organisational level.

In addition, the multidimensional approach (that follows from increased concerns of performance) has fuelled an increase in scope in which its many aspects are integrated as much as possible. Thus, parallel to the audit society, we suggest that it is possible to refer to a bourgeoning "control society" in which the role of control is increasing in both reach and scope and in which old solutions are mobilised to solve the problems that they have helped create. The question is: Does it make sense to retain our traditional thinking about control that was formed during a time when control models were the special province of a limited few? In the next section, we describe how it may be possible to achieve a balance among work demands, resources and support that facilitates control from the perspective of the controlled.

6.3 Enabling control with dialogue

Many control models are based on the information and control signals that people at the higher levels of the organisation send to people at the lower levels. However, information and control signals move in both directions in dialogue-based control. The dialogue is essential so that management can take responsibility for supporting people as they try to the balance the various organisational objectives. Messner (2009) explicitly calls for closer attention to the issue of responsibility when demands are issued. People who make demands should analyse the reasonableness of those demands as they consider the situation of the people who must satisfy those demands. This requires a dialogue that allows managers to understand such situations.

Of course, giving co-workers the opportunity in dialogue to influence demands may lead to a weakening of certain aspects of organisational strategy. Olve (1977) observes, however, that control is fundamentally a way to implement strategies intended to strengthen the organisation (see Chapter 2). The dilemma is the following: on the one hand, control of operations through dialogue risks weakening the possibility of making and implementing strategic decisions; on the other hand, rigid control with little or no dialogue risks failure in the sense that the controlled no longer solve problems creatively. Because of this dilemma, Olve emphasises that control requires dialogue in which the controlled are heard. Achieving this balance between offering the controlled a voice and establishing clear controls is the huge challenge in dialogue-based control because dialogue-based control certainly cannot be allowed to turn into inadequate control.

Responsibility can be demanded in various ways. Roberts (1991), in a discussion on the superiority of socially-based relationships that explain how accountability functions best, challenges the exclusive role of formal information in accountability. He favours dialogue. Messner (2009), who takes the same basic approach, argues that quantified information and specific routines, however, can be important – although in a different way. He writes:

> Standardization and quantification are not intrinsically problematic in ethical terms: rather, they are necessary forms of complexity reduction without which little could be achieved in practice.
>
> MESSNER, 2009, P. 923

Messner argues that control systems can (and perhaps should) use quantified information because of the common picture that numbers can illustrate. Numbers create opportunities to avoid the powerful evaluations that influence control too much or that question the boundaries of control. Adler and Borys (1996) describe a whole range of results from studies in which formal control systems support work by clarifying roles and responsibilities.

Numbers can be used to clarify such roles and responsibilities. However, this must be done in a new way – within the framework of a dialogue between hierarchical levels. While numbers and specific routes have an important, but not exclusive role, they provide support for dialogue. Olve (1977) argues that control is more complex and more nuanced than the traditional "command-and-control" logic. This point of view has undoubtedly gained ground. One of Olve's fundamental points is that the organisation's members have different (and not obviously compatible) interests. For that reason, he describes the purpose of dialogue as follows:

> ... to deal with uncombined multiple objectives, whose relations with one another become clarified during the planning process.
>
> OLVE, 1977, P. 12

6.4 Prerequisites for enabling control with dialogue

The control debate of today – and, we think, of tomorrow – is about the controlled and of the importance of dialogue. In this section we offer some ideas on a research field that we are convinced will receive greater attention in the future. From the perspective of the controlled, what is required for control to be understood as enabling their work?

Adler and Borys (1996) describe two types of bureaucratic control: coercive control and enabling control. Coercive control assumes that because people at work are opportunistic, supervisors should observe their actions and behaviour and check both actions and behaviour against appropriate standards. Therefore, when coercive control is used, the controlled may feel inhibited and compelled to work.

By contrast, enabling control puts formalisation into focus. Formalisation need not impose limitations on the controlled in a negative sense. Instead, formalisation means that the controlled are allowed to relate to their tasks and to see that they contribute to the organisation.

Ahrens and Chapman's (2004) study of control in a single-case field study of a restaurant reveals that although control models can often be both well-designed and well-developed, in practice control may be quite separate from the control model. This need not imply that the control models should be ignored as irrelevant. They suggest four design principles behind management control systems (repair, internal transparency, global transparency and flexibility) that constitute an enabling control system. The control model can be a point of

departure for a dialogue concerning what is a fair representation of organisational activities (repair). This dialogue, which is
based on the control system, may also create clarity about what
people are supposed to do (internal transparency) and how
their actions fit into the larger, organisational context (global
transparency). Ahrens and Chapman's study thus shows that
the separation of control from the control model need not be
problematic. Control models serve their purpose by establishing the game plan without creating negative restrictions
that prevent the controlled from doing good work (flexibility).

In Ahrens and Chapman's (2004) study, a flexible understanding of the control model and a dialogue on its limitations
are possible. What possibilities do the controlled have to participate in such dialogues? Jordan and Messner (2012) address this
issue in their study of the importance of how managers use
control. They point out that as long as the use of control is loose,
it can be seen as a way to create an image of the organisation to
which co-workers can relate. However, when the control indicators become accountable targets, and the control system shifts
from *enabling* to *coercive*, the controlled think these indicators
constrain them. Cushen (2013) reaches a similar conclusion in
a case study of how financial numbers create problems.

These studies – by Jordan and Messner (2012) and Cushen
(2013) – show the controlled can understand that numerical
representations are helpful if the numbers are used to create
a dialogue about the organisation rather than to exert strict
control over actions and behaviours. When people are evaluated solely on the basis of numbers, they lose confidence in
the numbers' power to measure their achievements. Every
variance is challenged as a possible deficiency. A less strict use

of numbers, in which the evaluation of a variance from the numbers is more nuanced, increases the likelihood of focusing on the positive aspects of numbers.[3]

Wouters and Wilderom (2008), in their study of performance-measurement systems, emphasise the centrality of their development and implementation processes. Control models that are based on organisational experience, testing and knowledge increase the potential for an enabling control. The controlled are more likely to think they are relevant to the organisation. Experience means, among other things, that people have a voice, and that they think the control system itself is relevant when it is implemented. The controlled have been involved in the implementation phase through dialogue. This dialogue, which allows the controlled to influence future events, may decrease their resistance to controls.

Cäker and Siverbo (2014), in their research on decentralised organisations, advance this discussion further. Their study shows that the resources available for control, especially time, are absolutely central. Dialogue-based control involves time spent communicating on control signals, especially the control signals that flow upward in the hierarchy. If organisations are designed with large span of control, with the number of subordinates approaching 50 or 100, the opportunity for dialogue-based control decreases. Although the managers continue to conduct formal meetings in which they listen to co-workers and

---

3 This reasoning suggests that different activities may require different management approaches. Organisations with strong qualitative elements, such as development activities or situations that require a high degree of flexibility, are often difficult to evaluate fairly. There is also a greater risk that accountability based on measurements may seem inadequate in comparison with simpler methods.

discuss uncertainties, these meetings can hardly substitute for the meetings in which small groups meet face-to-face.

However, co-workers under time pressure at work may not want to participate in dialogues, even when the opportunity exists. Cäker and Siverbo (2014) list two key aspects of successful dialogue:

1. the incentive for dialogue participation, and
2. confidence that managers listen to what the controlled say.

Regarding incentives, Cäker and Siverbo (2014) show that the dialogue on control has a role in the organisation's improvement work and that participation in dialogues is essential when new managers are appointed. They also observe that trust in managers is important for successful dialogues. It is difficult to imagine that co-workers want to engage in open dialogues with managers who are unlikely to listen to them or to follow through on the ideas discussed in the dialogues.

The participants in Cäker and Siverbo's (2014) study generally worked at the organisation for rather long periods, often years. Naturally, as time passed, they encountered the same people at various organisational levels. They got to know others rather well as they formed personal networks. Such networks often provide the incentive to create long-lasting dialogues. In his book on decision-making, Olve (1985, p. 83) also comments on the importance of cultivating "a network of personal contacts that provides the pieces of the puzzle that support an individual's own ideas" (translated from Swedish). Confidence in the future can increase the willingness of those who control, and of the controlled, to engage in dialogue.

6.5 Chapter conclusions

In this chapter, we emphasise the need to change the role of the controlled in management control processes. We argue that in today's organisations, a typical response to accountability legislation, the easy availability of IT applications and society's various demands is to produce more and more control information that relates to more and more organisational dimensions. As control increases, the controlled may face many conflicting objectives – to the point that they experience control overdose. We conclude that the early ideas on the dialogue between the controlling and the controlled are very relevant as such control increases. Organisations must conduct on-going dialogues around internal efficiencies (doing the right things in the right way) because control influences many of their dimensions and many of their people.

We suggest that such an approach to control requires that managers take increased responsibility for the reasonableness of management control systems. We recognise it is unlikely that everyone in an organisation will agree on a definition of what is a reasonable level since the controlled as a group are heterogeneous. Nevertheless, our intent in this chapter is to direct attention to the idea that the reasonableness of control merits discussion. The discussion should address control design, enabling control and dialogue. In particular, we emphasise the importance of incentives and trust among the controlled that gives them the confidence to send control signals "up" the organisation and thereby to create an environment receptive to meaningful dialogue.

References

Adler, Paul & Borys, Brian (1996). Two types of bureaucracy: Enabling and coercive. *Administrative Science Quarterly* 41(1), pp. 61–89.

Ahrens, Thomas & Chapman, Christopher S. (2004). Accounting for flexibility and efficiency: A field study of management accounting systems in a restaurant chain. *Contemporary Accounting Research* 21(2), pp. 271–301.

Ax, Christian & Bjørnenak, Trond (2005). Bundling and diffusion of management accounting innovation – the case of balanced scorecard in Sweden, *Management Accounting Research* 16(1), pp. 1–20.

Burchell, Stuart, Clubb, Colin, Hopwood, Anthony, Hughes, John & Nahapiet, Janine (1980). The roles of accounting in organizations and society. *Accounting, Organizations and Society* 5(1), pp. 5–27.

Catasús, Bino & Grönlund, Anders (2005). More peace for less money: Measurement and accountability in the Swedish Armed Forces. *Financial Accountability & Management* 21(4), pp. 467–484.

Cushen, Jean (2013). Financialization in the workplace: Hegemonic narratives, performative interventions and the angry knowledge worker. *Accounting, Organizations and Society* 38(4), pp. 314–331.

Cäker, Mikael (2007). Customer focus – an accountability dilemma. *European Accounting Review* 16(1), pp. 143–171.

Cäker, Mikael & Siverbo, Sven (2014). Strategic alignment in decentralized organizations – The case of Svenska Handelsbanken. *Scandinavian Journal of Management* 30(2), pp. 149–162.

Frow, Natalie, Marginson, David & Ogden, Stuart (2010). "Continuous" budgeting: Reconciling budget flexibility with budgetary control. *Accounting, Organizations and Society* 35(4), pp. 444–461.

Försäkringskassan (2015). *Stress vanligaste orsaken till sjukskrivning.* Press release, 1 April. Available at [http://goo.gl/OUIqvi] (Retrieved 2015-04-03).

Jensen, Michael C. & Meckling, William H. (1976). Theory of the firm: Managerial behavior, agency costs and ownership structure. *Journal of Financial Economics* 3(4), pp. 305–360.

Johanson, Ulf, Mårtensson, Maria & Skoog, Matti (2001). Mobilizing change through the management accounting of intangibles. *Accounting, Organizations and Society* 26(7), pp. 715–733.

Jordan, Silvia & Messner, Martin (2012). Enabling control and the problem of incomplete performance indicators. *Accounting, Organizations and Society* 37(8), pp. 544–564.

Kaplan, Robert & Johnson, Thomas (1987). *Relevance Lost: The Rise and Fall of Management Accounting*. Boston: Harvard Business School Press.

Kaplan, Robert & Norton, David (1996). *The Balanced Scorecard: Translating Strategy into Action*. Boston: Harvard Business School Press.

Lillis, Anne M. (2002). Managing multiple dimensions of manufacturing performance – an exploratory study. *Accounting, Organizations and Society* 27(6), pp. 497–529.

Messner, Martin (2009). The limits of accountability. *Accounting, Organizations and Society* 34(8), pp. 918–938.

Olve, Nils-Göran (1977). *Multiobjective Budgetary Planning: Models for Interactive Planning in Decentralized Organizations*. Doctoral thesis. Stockholm: Handelshögskolan.

Olve, Nils-Göran (1985). *Beslutsfattande. En tänkebok om rationella och irrationella beslut*. Stockholm: Liber förlag.

Olve, Nils-Göran, Roy, Jan & Wetter, Magnus (1997). *Balanced scorecard i svensk praktik: ledningsverktyg för strategisk verksamhetsstyrning*. Malmö: Liber.

Power, Michael (1999). *The Audit Society: Rituals of Verification*. Oxford: Oxford University Press.

Roberts, John (1991). The possibilities of accountability. *Accounting, Organizations and Society* 16(4), pp. 355–368.

Simons, Robert (1995). *Levers of Control: How Managers Use Innovative Control Systems to Drive Strategic Renewal*. Boston: Harvard Business School Press.

Wallander, Jan (1999). Budgeting – an unnecessary evil. *Scandinavian Journal of Management* 15(4), pp. 405–421.

Wouters, Marc & Wilderom, Celeste (2008). Developing performance-measurement systems as enabling formalization: A longitudinal field study of a logistics department. *Accounting, Organizations and Society* 33(4–5), pp. 488–516.

7. The controller's role

CECILIA GULLBERG & JAN LINDVALL

In this chapter, we examine the role of the controller (a key actor in management control) as a support for management in decision-making. We discuss how this role can be understood and strengthened in a number of organisational situations. In this discussion we also challenge traditional decision theory.

According to the Swedish Academy Dictionary, the word *styrekonom* should be used for this role. A relevant interpretation of the Academy's definition is that the controller (or *styrekonom*) is a co-worker with responsibility for an organisation's future-oriented, managerial control. According to Nils-Göran Olve, who has studied and influenced the role of the controller, particularly in the Swedish context, for some years, the word *"styrekonom"* describes the role very well (Olve, 2010).

However, in practice, the controller's role is not so clear or so well understood, and does not always have a focus on decision-making and future activities and events. As Robert Anthony, a pioneer in management control research, described the controller's role over 50 years ago, the role is multifaceted:

> In practice, people with the title of controller have functions that are, at one extreme, little more than bookkeeping and, at the other extreme, *de facto* general management.
>
> ANTHONY, 1965, P. 28; EMPHASIS IN THE ORIGINAL

Figure 7.1 shows the controller's role as a four-part matrix (Olve, 1988). The breadth of the role is illustrated by the number of information sources the controller works with (all relevant business information and accounting information) and by the number of groups of actors who use that information (the controllers and other interested parties, such as line managers). The controller's role varies depending on which dimensions are emphasised. The controller can have the following four roles:

- analyst
- coach
- accountant
- educator.

The commonality among the controller's four roles is that each role has a support function. The controller may provide this support, for example at the company's headquarters or on the factory floor. Thus, as Nilsson and Olve (2013, p. 22) state, the role of the controller as outlined in *Controllerhandboken* is "to support management in its control of the company" (translated from Swedish).

With the new organisational approaches, such as increased decentralisation, the controller's area of support has extended to other co-workers who make minor decisions and take actions daily that contribute to overall operational performance. Nevertheless, despite this broadening of the controller's role, the controller still performs the same basic function: to help the organisation set its goals and to help the organisation realise those goals.

Number of
information sources

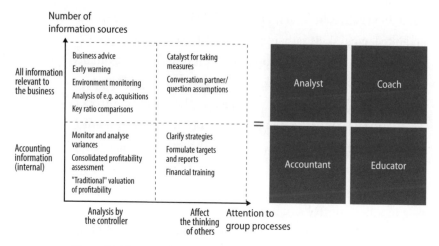

All information
relevant to
the business

Business advice
Early warning
Environment monitoring
Analysis of e.g. acquisitions
Key ratio comparisons

Catalyst for taking
measures
Conversation partner/
question assumptions

Accounting
information
(internal)

Monitor and analyse
variances
Consolidated profitability
assessment
"Traditional" valuation
of profitability

Clarify strategies
Formulate targets
and reports
Financial training

Analyst   Coach

Accountant   Educator

Analysis by
the controller

Affect
the thinking
of others

Attention to
group processes

Figure 7.1 The controller's four roles (representation of Nilsson et al., 2011,
p. 249). The left-hand side of the figure was first published in Olve, 1988, p. 14.

> Management control is the process by which managers assure that
> resources are obtained and used effectively and efficiently in the
> accomplishment of the organization's objectives.
>
> ANTHONY, 1965, P. 17

Based on Anthony's definition of management control we can
interpret the controller's work as something that occurs in
recurrent activities in which the main task is to support the
company's co-workers – the decision-makers – in ways that
produce, distribute and use resources in the best possible
way. All the controller's work is aimed at ultimately achieving
organisational goals.

To ensure the controller's work is performed consistently,
the structural aspects of the controller's work tasks, such as
rules, procedures and information systems, are often empha-

sised. In practice, however, as the knowledge economy expands and intellectual skills rather than physical materials and components become the basis of production, it is clear that *individuals' actions,* singly or together, can make an enormous difference in organisational performance. This also applies to the controller. As discussed later in the chapter, the controller's potential influence on line decisions and actions significantly depends on the controller's competence and personality (Olve, 1988).

With this background, we now focus on the controller's role in a key control situation: *the follow-up meeting.* In such meetings, the controller meets the line managers and other co-workers as they evaluate organisational performance and make decisions for the future.

Our discussion begins with a brief description of the follow-up meeting – what it means for the controller and why it is the focus of this chapter. Because the controller's primary task is to support line decision-making in various ways, including in follow-up meetings, we describe a few practical organisational situations that currently challenge traditional decision theory. These situations also place significant demands on the controller. Thereafter we describe these situations in greater detail, including their implications for the controller in the follow-up meeting. We summarise our observations in the chapter's conclusions.

7.1 The controller and the follow-up meeting: Decisions on achievements and actions

As stated in the previous section, formal structures are important in organisational control. Structures define and allocate responsibilities among the organisation's managers and co-workers. How extensive are these responsibilities? Do they apply only to costs? Or to both costs and revenues? Or to cash flows? Or to customer and co-worker satisfaction? With the increasing interest in tools such as the balanced scorecard (Kaplan & Norton, 1996; Olve et al., 2003), responsibility very typically includes both financial and non-financial elements.

Thus, responsibility structures are the foundation of the *on-going control processes*. These processes begin with setting goals and establishing standards of performance in the various responsibility areas. In this way, performance expectations are created. Then work begins on the planned activities. On their completion, the results of these activities are measured and evaluated in follow-up meetings. At this point, the original goals and standards are compared with the actual results. In this comparison of goals/standards with results, possible corrective actions and/or rewards for successful performance are discussed (Flamholtz, 1996).

During this process, decisions must be made on several occasions. One such occasion is the follow-up meeting in which evaluations of managers' performance are made and decisions are taken regarding future actions. Some decisions for future actions are made in response to negative variances from expected results. However, recent management control literature reflects a greater interest in evaluations of positive variances and the development of successful activities. For example, the term "interactive control" (Simons, 1995) is increasingly used to describe a more flexible approach to follow-up meetings and is now rather well-established and well-studied.

Whereas much time and energy are spent in setting goals

and making plans, following-up is at times somewhat over-looked. There are several reasons: not enough time, performance results are already known, and/or goals and standards are considered irrelevant (Gullberg, 2014). However, one need not conclude follow-up meetings are unimportant even though, in such cases, the form and content of the follow-up meeting very likely require some adjustment.

We think the controller – who typically produces a large number of reports and key figures with the intention of monitoring activities in various dimensions – has an important role in making follow-up meetings more interesting and more instructive. Of course, the controller is also a participant in other decision-making situations in the on-going management control process (e.g. in planning meetings or in informal work conversations). However, the controller's role in the follow-up meeting is especially important.

The controller often has a central role in the creation and interpretation of information that is the basis of follow-up meetings. Briefly, the controller's work can be said to include everything from manual transfer of information between different systems to presentations of results with reference to overall goals, including clarifications of financial concepts. Furthermore, the controller may be active in establishing the standards used in the performance comparisons (such as standards related to budgets and to historic costs and other costs/values). The controller may also assist in analysing and explaining variances from standards. As indicated in Figure 7.1 there are different controller roles, and therefore the above-mentioned activities may be emphasised to a different extent by different controllers.

Next we describe some important aspects of decision-making and their implications for the controller's role in the follow-up meeting.

7.2 A changed practice places new demands on decision theory – and on the controller

In the previous section we reviewed an important control situation and what it means in terms of organisational decisions and the controller's role in those decisions. We argued that the follow-up meeting, consistent with fundamental control principles, can produce a number of decisions that lead to action. For example, the controller's variance analysis may show that the company's actual pricing profile differs from its planned pricing profile. Now we will describe how some emerging organisational situations challenge traditional decision-making theory.

A significant part of the normative academic commentary on organisational decision-making is based on assumptions and ideal types – with limited empirical support. Empirical decision research – both experiments and case studies of real decision-making situations – takes a different perspective. For example, in his book *Thinking, Fast and Slow*, Daniel Kahneman (2011) admits that using rapid, intuitive and emotional reasoning and taking action based on rules of thumb are sometimes appropriate. However, he argues that slower, more thoughtful analysis in decision-making is also needed. Kahneman, who is a psychologist and behavioural scientist, was awarded the 2002 Nobel Memorial Prize in Economic Sciences for his empirical research on people's non-rational behaviour. In some ways this research challenges the very core of economic decision-making theory. Olve (1985) has also argued, with specific regard to management control, that managers should dare to venture outside the rational sphere, even by acting on intuition. In general, there is increasing interest in how insights on decisions and actions can provide individual, organisational and social solutions that improve the conditions needed for good behaviour in the long term.

The relevance of these ideas about how to think is that the controller, whose work largely involves explaining operations to relevant decision-makers using numbers, may need to consider some less analytical methods of conveying information. Therefore, the focus of this section is the controller's need to understand the importance of both ways of thinking about decisions.

We discuss the following three ideas on decision-making:

- A group of people, rather than a single individual, makes many decisions.

- Decisions are not necessarily made at a single point in time; often they are made at the end of a longer, on-going process of anchoring.

- Support for decisions is not easily calculated. Therefore, the possible outcomes of various decision alternatives are unclear. Even when there is clarity, consensus is rarely certain on the choice of alternatives. Thus, decisions are usually characterised by the complexity of the cause-and-effect results related to the various alternatives and by different priorities.

Such practical observations on decision-making contrast sharply with the theory of individual decision-making in which one person, at one time, makes an informed and knowledgeable decision – a decision that can easily be supported with calculations prepared according to generally accepted priorities.

7.2.1 Individual decisions or group decisions?

Traditional decision theory stems from the idea of the individual decision-maker. However, many people today are more inclined to support the idea that decisions are made collectively, in groups. At present, more and more organisations use projects and teams for their activities. Often conflicting objectives that require compromises characterise such groups. Even in activities that are organised more traditionally, one finds collective decision-making. The controller, for example, works collectively with the line managers in follow-up meetings where results are discussed and future actions are planned. Moreover, there is evidence that a group in a difficult decision situation tends to homogenise as the members seek a simplified consensus decision. Thereafter, the group has difficulty in absorbing new, conflicting information even when such information would be of value for the decisions.

On the one hand, when a decision involves several people (as opposed to only one decision-maker), the situation may lead to different interpretative frames. On the other hand, the possibility of explicit social pressure within the group may influence these interpretations.

On the one hand, accounting information presented at a follow-up meeting may result in various interpretations of the organisation's performance and various recommendations for possible actions. Consider the following scenario. "Are we satisfied with a project return of 19 million?" "Not really," according to the controller, since 20 million was expected. "Yes," according to the project manager who has experienced multiple project delivery delays and conflicts and who has mentally adjusted the return downward. "No," according to the project manager's manager who knows that similar projects have produced larger returns. On the other hand, social pressure within the group at the follow-up meetings may downplay some of these interpretations.

The controller should do more than simply distribute the accounting information at the follow-up meeting in the expectation that such information by itself will explain the results and suggest action. Instead, the controller should take an active role in the meeting by encouraging participants to express their opinions, by explaining the accounting information from different points of view, and by describing possible future actions. In this role, the controller is an educator who explains data to co-workers and a coach who encourages co-workers to re-think their assumptions and offer suggestions. Controllers should even challenge their own assumptions, for example concerning the need for strict budgetary compliance. Insisting on strict budgetary compliance tends to render line managers less flexible and open to opportunities and may, at least in a turbulent business environment, result in lost opportunities (Jannesson et al., 2014).

7.2.2 Decision points or decision processes?

Although traditional decision theory is forward-looking (e.g. as in its approach to "sunk costs" that ignores costs already incurred), there are scholars who recognise that decisions sometimes evolve gradually. For example, Nutt (2007) has explained how difficult it is to make good decisions when there are carryover problems from a previous stage. In many cases, these problems result from incorrect assumptions or flawed information collection. Once decision support is presented in a follow-up meeting it is already influenced by these previous assumptions, and therefore the choice among alternatives can generally be taken for granted. Thus, decisions can be seen as processes in which the potential for exerting influence may be greatest in the introductory phase. In other words, decisions evolve rather than spring up at a particular point in time.

Decisions that evolve, step by step, are not necessarily taken at follow-up meetings. One reason is that company management may not particularly prioritise such meetings. Line managers, for example, sometimes have limited interest in the information the controller presents at follow-up meetings. Among other things, their perception may be that such meetings are not an efficient use of their time. Line managers who work closely with operations generally have a rather good understanding of the progress of operations long before the follow-up meeting. They know if costs exceed budget, if co-workers have good work morale, or if there are quality variances. They may not be able to quantify this knowledge exactly, but they have a rather good grasp of the general situation (Van der Veeken & Wouters, 2002; Gullberg, 2014).

Given this understanding, line managers can make decisions in on-going operations in advance of the presentation of reports at follow-up meetings. Thus, the important task of controllers is to embrace the roles of educator and coach in order to be able to contribute to the evolutionary process of decision-making.

The controller should always take an active role in analysing the organisation's operations. Although line managers may have a fairly good understanding of current operations, they may be surprised by the new facts, impressions and trends that the controller presents. The controller's analysis, for example, can reveal which customer groups and which product groups are most profitable, or how purchase prices vary from supplier to supplier. Such data, which sheds light on operations, may ultimately influence the decisions taken in follow-up meetings. Because, as noted above, line managers do not always prioritise such analyses, the controller should be proactive in presenting accounting information, some of which may challenge existing ideas.

The controller should also be involved in the preparation and discussion of goals and standards. As mentioned above, the comparisons between actual and projected amounts may sometimes be perceived as irrelevant. For example, when operating and surrounding conditions change, the budgeted amounts calculated some months previously may no longer seem reasonable. Or comparisons (benchmarks) with different units, departments, or competitors may seem unfair because conditions are not the same everywhere (see the discussion of the controlled co-workers' perspective in Chapter 6). When resistance to such comparisons arises, the risk is that the company will simply continue along the same uninspired path.

One way to handle this risk is to work more actively to create relevant goals and standards. One possibility is to use the "rolling budget", in which budgeted amounts are continuously updated as changes in the operations occur. Another possibility is to focus on comparisons with entities operating under similar conditions. Yet another possibility is to hold discussions on the goals and standards in order to understand why they are perceived as irrelevant and to determine whether specific parts of a budget could still be relevant as standards for comparison.

These actions can be taken in well-prepared, fact-based discussions in follow-up meetings or by the dissemination of regular reports that include follow-up commentary. Cieślak (2011) concludes that regular communications between controllers and line managers are essential in order that the controller is seen as a "fellow player" who has the coach/educator role. In essence, we believe that the controller should make every effort to continuously contribute to decision-making rather than wait for the formal decision-making occasions.

7.2.3 Fact-based or value-oriented decisions?

As stated above, it is not entirely clear which interpretation of the information presented in the follow-up meeting is correct. For this reason, a discussion is needed to understand not only the actual facts but also the relevant values that need to be weighed against each other prior to making decisions. Herbert Simon (1945/1976) makes a clear distinction between decisions based on facts and decisions based on value judgments – sometimes described as programmed decisions and non-programmed decisions. James March (1994), a colleague of Simons, makes a similar distinction between two decision-making logics: the logic of consequences and the logic of appropriateness.

In essence, both Simons and March are writing about two kinds of decisions: fact-based (i.e. calculated) decisions and value-oriented decisions. Fact-based decisions are based on clear cause-effect relationships in which it is possible to apply reason in choosing which course of action is the most useful. Value-oriented decisions are based on what is assumed legitimate – from one's own perspective and/or from that of others. Given the complexity of organisations – most easily seen by the impossibility of relying entirely on calculations in many decision situations – our need for value-oriented decisions increases. According to March (1994), a number of critical questions arise in making such complex, value-oriented decisions. Who am I? What is this situation? What would someone like me do in a situation like this?

Thus, both the situation and the individual (who is closely related to a professional identity) can influence value-oriented decisions. Empirical evidence shows that decision-making is often less utility-centred than the traditional decision models assume. In many situations, the legitimacy of the final outcome is more important.

Some decisions are more difficult because of the presence of more accounting information – more in amount as well as in complexity. This is observable with the increase in control models aimed at strengthening and broadening our decision-making powers. The use of future-oriented performance models such as Economic Value Added and Key Performance Indicators, and of multidimensional models such as the Balanced Scorecard, increases the possibility that the decision-support points in various directions.

For example, the expectation of today that people will act in ways that are more environmentally friendly and more ethical is stronger than it has been for many years. Of course, at least in the short term, such conduct, if achieved, is likely to have a monetary cost. How should we compare results between projects that respect the environment and those that do not? Should projects that are less profitable but more environmentally friendly be rewarded in some way even though they are more costly? Another example is customer relationship management; to what extent should customers have a voice, especially if they advocate actions that are likely to decrease our profit margin? Are we willing to sacrifice customer goodwill to save money?

These are questions that cannot be answered easily with numbers. They must be discussed in terms of competing values whenever they arise. Clearly some people think the way to address such questions is with financial calculations that produce the "right" answer. Yet many controllers and line managers are more inclined to think such complex questions merit a thoughtful, value-oriented discussion using the logic of appropriateness. The strategy map (see Chapter 2) is useful for weighing up the pros and cons of such trade-offs.

We conclude that the controller who sits in the accountant's "safe corner" (Olve, 1988) should expand this role to that of the coach. Controllers should not limit their understanding to financial information; they need a good grasp of non-financial information (reflecting, for example, company values, goals and strategies) and how it relates to the financial dimension. A narrow focus on the company's financial dimension is likely to decrease the chances for fruitful dialogues between controller and line managers. Furthermore, reasoning from a wide set of numerical indicators is insufficient; controllers also need to reason without numbers.

7.3 The controller's balance between reason and emotion

The controller is often an essential player in the organisation's management control activities as Robert Anthony explained as far back as 1965 in his discussion of the controller's role. For example, he underlined the controller's responsibility for the development and use of the organisation's information systems (Anthony, 1965). Line managers today also use such systems for reporting and retrieving data. However, despite this hybridisation of the roles of the controller and line manager (cf. Scapens & Jazayeri, 2003), the controller still has an important role in both the development and use of information systems – systems that are an ever important part of the organisation's control system.

As previously noted, the reliance on non-financial data in organisations is increasing. Therefore controllers who dare to work with non-financial data and engage in discussions with line managers are well positioned to take a major role in the organisation's management control activities.

We propose that defining management control and the controller's work solely in terms of numerical data retrieved from information systems has certain limitations. These views are limited because they are narrowly based on the intellectual, or reason-based, perspective. Without denying the importance of this perspective, we claim management control (and the controller) should also recognise the importance of other aspects of human behaviour. This conclusion is consistent with the claims in previous studies that the controller should be a competent communicator who understands group dynamics (Sathe, 1982; Olve, 1988; Lindvall, 2009).

In previous sections we examined three aspects of decision-making, as well as the challenges they present for the controller. These challenges involve social processes related to interpretative frames, values and motivations in decision-making in which the controller should take a proactive role as educator or coach. In the next two sub-sections we develop these ideas in order to capture some aspects of the controller's work that we think are especially important for these roles in which the combination of "hard" and "soft" elements – that is, "Sense (reason) and Sensibility (emotion)" – is essential.

7.3.1 Words are necessary for understanding and using numbers

As is clearly evident, numbers are a central part of the organisation's control system: numbers are intended to focus our attention on the organisation's operations. In the area of management control, one of the most widely known axioms is "What gets measured gets done", or, as Kaplan and Norton (1996, p. 21) write, "If you can't measure it, you can't manage it." More goals, more metrics and more reports are often responses to a weak focus on important operational questions. However, there is a risk that new problems will arise (see Chapter 6). Herbert Simon (1993), recipient of the 1978 Nobel Memorial Prize in Economic Sciences, concluded that a wealth of information poses the risk of creating poverty in attention.

In addition, there is the risk that people only measure what is easy to measure, resulting in a skewed representation of reality at the expense of certain aspects that may not be easily quantified. Furthermore, as mentioned, different people may interpret the same number, such as a project's financial results, in various ways and the increasing use of multidimensional metrics may point in different directions.

Overall, there are thus a number of indications that controllers, in their roles as coach or educator for line managers, should present only a reasonable display of numbers. Furthermore, these numbers should increase the line managers' understanding of operational activities as well as draw their attention to relevant areas. Numbers and words should be combined in such a way that the various metrics mesh with the line managers' verbal descriptions of activities and provide a more complete picture. (See Chapter 2 on the importance of narratives in strategy work).

At the beginning of multiyear projects, uncertainty often exists as far as setting reasonable targets, establishing timeframes, and projecting financial results are concerned. For example, how a project unfolds depends a great deal on customer relationships, on agreements on deliverables, etc. Thus, at follow-up meetings, it is advisable to examine how relationships with customers have worked thus far in the project and how they are expected to work in the near future. Are there current problems with the customer such as disputed payments for cost overruns? Are there other potential sources of disturbance that may jeopardise the goals of the project? Without doubt, these narratives contribute to a more comprehensive picture than if only numbers are used to describe the status of a project. The controller should ask the line managers questions and then consider their answers when future actions are discussed.

Of course, narratives can introduce difficulties when entities are compared. However, metrics can also pose difficulties if the situations between the compared entities differ. The advantage of a narrative is that it offers a more vivid, more nuanced and richer description of a particular situation than numbers, used without words, can. Therefore, narratives, when combined with numbers at follow-up meetings, could divert managers from justifying their insufficient performance and instead focusing attention on several possible explanations, lessons learned, and possible new objectives and expectations. The use of both numbers and words in evaluating performance and deciding on future actions means that the controller and the line managers should relax some controls (e.g. the frequency and the scope of the follow-up) and instead trust the co-workers' ability to deliver good results.

An on-going, and related, discussion in Sweden today concerns whether public sector professionals (e.g. teachers and doctors) need more flexibility in their work. One of the main issues in this discussion is control. Would such professionals benefit from controls other than numerical metrics and detailed rules?[1] Also in the private sector, since at least the early 1990s, the trend in Sweden is to use looser controls that give co-workers greater flexibility in responding to unplanned-for problems. Because the choice of control models is rarely a matter of either-or, the controller must consult with line managers who understand the operations, the situation, and the co-workers' personalities and attitudes. With this understanding, the right kind and the right amount of control can be exercised.

Making room for work-related narratives can pose a challenge for the controller who works mainly with numbers. Many controllers, especially those who emphasise their roles as accountant and analyst, are quite distant from the line managers' issues and concerns. Therefore, controllers may have a rather limited understanding of the operational activities. They find that numbers are a safe way to exercise control over operations and a comfortable language to use in discussing results – despite the fact that more supportive and stimulating approaches to managing/evaluating activities are possible. On the other hand, narratives can help the controller achieve further insights into activities.

7.3.2 Analysis and energy bring finance and operations closer

As discussed previously in this chapter, some decisions are made in part before the formal, underlying decision data have

---

1 The government policy statement (Fall, 2014, p. 12) states, among other things: "The professions in the public sector must be strengthened. New control models will be developed that create more freedom for public sector co-workers" (translated from Swedish).

been presented. One explanation for this situation may be that many line managers think accounting information does not add much that is new (Van der Veeken & Wouters, 2002; Gullberg, 2014). Moreover, people on the organisation's accounting staff are often described as "bean counters". This rather negative epithet is used for people who are thought to focus joylessly and single-mindedly on numbers to the exclusion of all else. In this context, the former CEO of Swedish TV 4, Jan Scherman (2014), described a conversation he had with a glass artist at Kosta Boda, a well-known Swedish glass manufacturer:

> A glass artist, who was frustrated with the new developments at the glassworks, exclaimed angrily: "Now every sculpture, bowl, candlestick holder – even the smallest object – has to have a project number and an income statement. The controller wants a written plan with costs and revenues. It is the same with every exhibition – a business plan and a marketing plan are required. Estimated sales, estimated warehouse costs. The number of firsts and the number of seconds. Out with energy, joy and imagination. In with profit and loss statements." [Translated from Swedish]

Thus, because the perception of "finance" differs from the perception of "operations", a certain amount of scepticism surrounds the issues that controllers deal with and the information they produce. It is unsurprising that follow-up meetings often feature what Gratton and Ghoshal (2002) describe as "dehydrated talk". Such dialogues are conducted in a ritualistic manner in which the participants talk about familiar and/or rather uninteresting and uncontroversial subjects. Important control-related dialgues, when held this way, can cause serious, long-term damage to the organisation's management control system. When such dialogues are perceived as boring and unimportant, they do not attract much attention and do not invite participation (Simon, 1993). According to Gratton and Ghoshal (2002), follow-up meetings should be characterised by both analytical depth and emotional energy. Even if "it takes two to tango", the controller, especially in the role of coach or educator, certainly has the potential to build the commitment and create the enthusiasm needed to conduct such follow-up meetings.

One possible explanation for this lack of interest in follow-up meetings is that some line managers do not really understand their financial responsibility or the financial relationships in operations. Instead of trying to learn the language of accounting/finance, they dismiss some issues as boring. They prefer to hand these issues over to the "delegated" accountant. For example, line managers sometimes think that accountants make simple things unnecessarily complicated.

However, what is overlooked when this attitude is taken is that finance/accounting deals with more than the total of specific positive and negative numbers. In fact, the accountant's calculations involve many estimates and adjustments that require an understanding of a variety of financial as well as operational terms. Thus, the controller needs to train the line managers with regard to definitions, reporting procedures and the relationships between the various operational dimensions.

Another explanation for the lack of interest in follow-up meetings may be the deficiencies in how control information is communicated. Even if line managers appreciate the role of finance/accounting in the organisation, they may think they receive accounting information too late to be useful. They may also think this information is too aggregated to provide any useful insights into operations. It is not surprising that such people are reluctant to participate in follow-up meetings. Furthermore, accounting information may sometimes require manual production and reporting by line managers, thus competing with other important managerial tasks (Gullberg, 2014).

A frequently stated reason for these problems is that information systems have not enabled frequent and detailed analyses – although, given the development of more sophisticated information systems, this is changing. For example, in a management control-related change project, a large Swedish company strongly emphasised the importance of making accounting information more appealing. The idea was to make the information easier to report and retrieve, and to make it more relevant by the use of "tailor-made" versions that included both financial and non-financial data.

As line managers use these new technologies, they may take greater interest in follow-up meetings and may better prepare for them. However, it is important to understand that the development and analysis of accounting information is only one of many managerial activities – all of which compete for a share of people's time, regardless of the interest level. It is therefore reasonable to conclude that the controller – despite the new technologies – should support the management of accounting information. The controller could spark interest in follow-up meetings by other means. We noted some ideas in this respect earlier in the chapter: encouraging storytelling, challenging assumptions, and highlighting different, and sometimes conflicting, perspectives. In this way, the controller can provoke analytical reasoning and high energy among the participants at follow-up meetings.

7.4 Chapter conclusions

This chapter features an essential player in the organisation's management control system – the controller. Our focus is the follow-up meeting – a control situation in which activities (projects, etc.) are evaluated on the basis of information. Line managers, together with the controller, evaluate the performance of their subordinates and decide on future actions.

The chapter also examines a number of organisational situations that, contrary to traditional decision theory, suggest that decisions often involve social processes related to interpretative frames, organisational values and human motivation. These processes are realities that place special demands on the controller. We argue that the controller should consider these realities in his/her work and not be led astray by theoretical (and unrealistic) assumptions that can create frustration. In so doing, the controller to a large extent assumes the roles of coach and educator (Olve, 1988). In these roles, they help develop goals and standards, identify business relationships, and question long-held ideas.

This requires the controller to create and maintain a balance between reason and emotion (i.e. "sense and sensibility"). By reason, we mean the recognition that accounting information, which is produced for follow-up meetings, should be factual and of high quality. By emotion, we mean the recognition that accounting information should be presented in appealing, accessible ways that encourage discussion, personal experience narratives, and differences of opinion in order to enhance meaningfulness and spark motivation.

We admit that many controllers have not assumed the coach and educator roles. Every organisation has its own technical and operational situation, and not all situations support the controller in these roles – or necessitate that the controller fully assumes these roles. Nevertheless, in consideration of how decisions are made in practice, we support the idea that organisations benefit from broadening the controller role as we have described. With more informative and more engaging discussions of accounting information at follow-up meetings, controllers benefit, line managers benefit, and perhaps most important, organisations benefit.

References

Anthony, Robert N. (1965). *Planning and Control Systems: A Framework for Analysis*. Boston: Harvard University Graduate School of Business Administration.

Cieślak, Katarzyna (2011). *The Work of the Accounting & Controlling Department and its Drivers*. Doctoral thesis. Lund: Lund Business Press.

Flamholtz, Eric G. (1996). Effective organizational control: A framework, applications and implications. *European Management Journal* 14(6), pp. 596–611.

Gratton, Lynda & Ghoshal, Sumantra (2002). Improving the quality of conversations. *Organizational Dynamics* 31(3), pp. 209–223.

Gullberg, Cecilia (2014). *Roles of Accounting Information in Managerial Work*. Doctoral thesis. Uppsala: Uppsala universitet.

Jannesson, Erik, Nilsson, Fredrik & Rapp, Birger (Eds.) (2014). *Strategy, Control and Competitive Advantage: Case Study Evidence*. Berlin/ Heidelberg: Springer.

Kahneman, Daniel (2011). *Thinking, Fast and Slow*. New York: Farrar, Strauss and Giroux.

Kaplan, Robert S. & Norton, David P. (1996). *The Balanced Scorecard: Translating Strategy into Action*. Boston: Harvard Business School Press.

Lindvall, Jan (2009). *Controllerns nya roll: Om verksamhetsstyrning i informationsrik miljö*. Stockholm: Norstedts.

March, James G. (1994). *A Primer on Decision Making. How Decisions Happen*. New York: Free Press.

Nilsson, Fredrik & Olve, Nils-Göran (2013). Ekonomistyrning och controllerns roll. In: Nilsson, Fredrik & Olve, Nils-Göran (Eds.), *Controllerhandboken*. Stockholm: Liber, pp. 19–27.

Nilsson, Fredrik, Olve, Nils-Göran & Parment, Anders (2011). *Controlling for Competitiveness: Strategy Formulation and Implementation through Management Control*. Malmö: Liber.

Nutt, Paul C. (2007). Intelligence gathering for decision making. *Omega* 35(5), pp. 604–622.

Olve, Nils-Göran (1985). *Beslutsfattande – en tänkebok om rationella och intuitiva beslut*. Lund: Liber.

Olve, Nils-Göran (1988). *Controllerns roll – konturer av en affärsekonom*. Stockholm: Mekanförbundets förlag.

Olve, Nils-Göran (2010). *Gästkrönika: hellre "styrekonom" än "controller"*. CFO World, 18 May 2010, available at [http://cfoworld. idg.se/2.13965/1.320127/gastkronika-hellre-styrekonom-an-controller] (Retrieved 2016-01-26).

Olve, Nils-Göran, Petri, Carl-Johan, Roy, Jan & Roy, Sofie (2003). *Making Scorecards Actionable – Balancing Strategy and Control*. London: John Wiley & Sons.

Sathe, Vijay (1982). *Controller Involvement in Management*. Englewood Cliffs: Prentice Hall.

Scapens, Robert & Jazayeri, Mostafa (2003). ERP systems and management accounting change: opportunities or impacts? A research note. *European Accounting Review* 12(1), pp. 201–233.

Scherman, Jan (2014). *Räkna med känslorna - tankar från en murvel som blev börs-vd*. Stockholm: Norstedts.

Simon, Herbert A. (1945/1976). *Administrative Behavior. A Study of Decision-Making Processes in Administrative Organization*. New York: Free Press.

Simon, Herbert A. (1993). *Reason in Human Affairs*. Stanford: Stanford University Press.

Simons, Robert (1995). Control in an age of empowerment. *Harvard Business Review* 73(2), pp. 80–88.

The government policy statement (2014). Regeringsförklaringen. Available at [www.regeringen.se/content/1/c6/24/71/20/9d251590.pdf] (Retrieved 2016-08-28).

Van der Veeken, Henk J. M. & Wouters, Mark J. F. (2002). Using accounting information systems by operations managers in a project company. *Management Accounting Research* 13(3), pp. 45–370.

8. Conclusions

ALF WESTELIUS, CARL-JOHAN PETRI
& FREDRIK NILSSON

Strategic Management Control deals with how control supports the organisation's strategy. At first glance, this statement seems almost self-evidently true. Few people are likely to claim their organisation lacks a control system aimed at supporting the work of designing and implementing strategy. In practice, however, people encounter many difficulties and challenges in exercising management control strategically. Surprisingly, at many companies the management control system is very traditional in its design – despite more than three decades of debate on "how to be relevant" – or, as proposed in this book, "how to be strategic". However, some literature points to examples of the positive effects of strategic management control on how an organisation develops. The issue is unresolved, and both researchers and practitioners are still interested in strategic management control. There is thus a need to continue analysing and discussing what makes management control strategic. One purpose of this book is to contribute to this important discussion.

The description of management control processes in textbooks inspires the structure of this book: planning and following-up. Within this overarching structure, our ambition in this book is to present a coherent picture, encompassing areas that we think have particular relevance in the discussion of strategic management control. In Chapters 2 to 7, the authors examine several classic control concepts related to metrics, decisions and responsibility, as well as several more recent concepts that have significant influence, such as control package, control mix and strategy maps. The structure of management control receives considerable attention, but the importance of actors is also emphasised. This shows in the centrality awarded to the need for more organisational dialogue and more engaging, vivid narratives. Although the theme of how to design and use management control to fit a certain strategy is important, we have chosen to allot little space to it. Since it has been treated extensively and in detail in many other texts, we decided to devote the main part of our attention to other relevant issues.

One of the book's conclusions is that the strategy should be visible and understandable if it is to permeate the entire organisation. Co-workers throughout the organisation, whatever their hierarchical level, should be able to explain the organisation's strategy to others (see Chapter 2). Those who want others to buy into their view on what is "the relevant organisation" – the unit that is to be controlled – need to present a credible and persuasive story of what and why (see Chapter 3). Both managers and co-workers should initiate strategic dialogues within the management control framework to ensure that the everyday activities are both guided by the strategy, and can provide impulses for changes in organisational focus (see Chapter 4).

Product costing is a central tool in traditional management control literature. However, since the 1990s, critics have charged that this costing literature, with its primary focus on the organisation's costs, is too inward-looking. They claim that selling prices should be based on the product's value to the customer. Chapter 5 provided an example of how the organisation's pricing and costing models could link with its overall strategy.

As management control is expected to replace direct instructions in guiding the actions of increasing portions of the workforce, at ever lower hierarchical levels, and more remote from the organisation's top management, the importance of mutual dialogue between managers and co-workers will increase. These dialogues may, for example, focus on the reasonableness of achieving specified goals. Such dialogues are important parts in creating a perception of management control as a support and not as a straitjacket (see Chapter 6). Moreover, controllers should play an active and significant role in strategic management control by dressing their analyses in practice-relevant narratives, not just in numbers. Then they can address both emotions and rationality, and more effectively support their counterparts (see Chapter 7).

A central theme of the book is the need for dialogues, both on the content of the strategy (in order to craft, disseminate and explain it) and on how it is implemented using, for example, strategy maps, balanced scorecards and narratives. The management control literature does not often describe cinematic science as the inspiration for strategy and control work. However, we think controllers would do well to look for inspiration in such unconventional sources. Since at least the early 1990s, practitioners and researchers have recommended the benefits of using narratives (storytelling) in the business world. Why, then, should strategic management control cling to formal programmes and graphs if the goal is to involve as many people as possible and to make strategic control issues relevant in everyday work life? It follows that controllers should learn to use emotional emphasis to convey management control insights in an engaging way. And those who are expected to work committedly, form independent decisions and work towards set goals should also participate in the strategic dialogues concerning which the goals are, if the targets are achievable, and how the goals can be reached.

Managers and co-workers should be involved in the work on strategy regardless of whether the organisation prioritises financial goals or other goals. Whether the primary goals are financial or not is often assumed to depend on what sector the organisation operates in (for-profit, not-for-profit, or public). While the book does not address this issue directly, that assumption is questionable. The strategic dialogues – given the tools and the actors this book describes – may very well cause a hi-tech company to choose the development of sophisticated and elegant technology as its main goal, and view financial performance as a restriction that must be met to be able to continue striving for technical elegance. As another example, consider staff at a private school who agree their main goals are to promote learning and to contribute to the fostering of educated and reflective children and adolescents, but are subject to achieving a profitability that allows them to continue achieving these goals in the long term. Look around. Despite the current emphasis on quarterly financial results and shareholder value, many people are motivated by pride in doing a job well, community involvement, care, friendship or curiosity. Should the organisation's strategy map more clearly reflect such values, or should they mainly enter the discussions about the map and the management control?

In the book we also observe it has become increasingly less clear what unit "the relevant organisation" refers to. Various networking structures, collaborations, and partnerships make organisational boundaries areas for discussion and decision-making rather than clearly defined territories. While the management control literature has engaged with this idea for some time, the discussion may be even more intense in other fields. Partly by drawing on other fields, such as marketing and strategy, we have attempted to demonstrate relatedness and differences between various traditions that deal with "the relevant organisation". Primarily, the traditions differ in ambition to focus on that which is nearby (and easy to overview), and that which is more distant and yet is part of the interactions and influences that surround one's own organisation. The message is that it is to some extent possible to evaluate, coordinate and control an area larger than one's own organisation. However, sometimes there may be a reason to focus on the clarity and tangibility of the more narrowly delimited, with fewer – and because of that, perhaps also stronger – goals and ambitions.

Controllability is related to the possibility of evaluation. People given responsibility should have access to metrics that make it possible both for the person responsible to act to fulfil the goals, and for others to assess how the responsibility has been handled. However, a single, reflective individual, or a group of such people in total agreement, seldom design the organisation and its goals. Organisations, their strategies and control systems evolve through the decisions and actions of many people. Even the lone individual has difficulty, at least in the long term, in maintaining consistency in thought and action. For these reasons, control tools and control systems often fail to provide clear and consistent signals. In Chapter 4, Jannesson and Nilsson present strategic congruence and integrated control as the ideal. It would certainly be simpler for actors if goals were clear and unambiguous, and if the control signals pointed in the same direction. Although examples of such goals and signals exist in management and research literature, far fewer examples are found in reality. Therefore, the strategic dialogues, with their on-going discussion on different interpretations of control signals, on the priorities among possible actions, and on the strategic bets for an uncertain future, are increasingly important. Without such discussions that include reconciliations of opposing views, joint sense-making and the development of agreed-on interpretations, the flora of organisational actions would be unkempt.

In unstable environments, it may be an advantage that management control is not so unified and unambiguous that it gives the impression that there is only one true and clearly defined path – that path could prove to lead in the wrong direction. However, most people probably agree the control mix indicating desired paths works better if it is more planned and coordinated than if it is completely haphazard. However, most large organisations today probably use more control tools than are needed or desired. Strategic management control is about selecting and rejecting. Rather than constantly adding new control tools and enriching others, it may be more beneficial, continuing with our nature metaphor, to prune some of the overgrowth.

In Chapter 6, Catasús and Cäker, in taking the perspective of the controlled, address the frustration and confusion among co-workers caused by increasingly comprehensive control systems; systems that are not only to be interpreted and adhered to, but also fed with data and assessments. Ever-increasing control may simply be unproductive. Control systems which, through metrics, are intended to provide people far from the actual operations with a sense of information and control, are not necessarily effective components of well-functioning strategic management control. The importance of a dialogue on control reappears. From this viewpoint, both the controlling and the controlled (on many connected levels) should build a common understanding of meaningful control and of realistic and appropriate goals. Such dialogues help managers and co-workers see their differences, the bases for these differences, and the possibilities for reconciliation of divergent ideas.

In Chapter 7, Gullberg and Lindvall argue that the structured images created in follow-up meetings, based on retrospective evaluations and the forward-looking analyses that control systems enable, are undervalued assets. They decline to blame line managers and co-workers entirely for this situation, and point to the controller's role as an important resource for analysing, interpreting and including metrics-based control signals in discussions about the business' results and future direction. Follow-up meetings offer the controller a clear setting for entering the collective decision-making that permeates operations. A controller with an overview, analytical skill, business knowledge, empathy and rhetoric talent can, of course, be a great asset. However, also controllers that do not possess this grand repertoire of experiences or skills can develop into important players in the organisation's control mix. In such a position, a well-prepared and convincing controller can be influential – not least due to the status of "fact-based control". It is, then, important to remember that financial measurements and calculations are always approximations and represent somebody's assessment, not absolute truths. And the controller needs to play the role responsibly.

The suggestive capacity of numbers, rather than their ability to present final truths, is also pointed out by Ax, Cöster and Iveroth in Chapter 5, when they discuss costing and pricing. Pricing, which can involve strategic betting, can benefit from discussions that lead to mutually satisfying, or at least acceptable, solutions. Cost calculations, which are often the basis of pricing decisions, always depend on assumptions about causation and on partially arbitrary allocations. The value-based cost analysis that the authors present can therefore serve as an interesting contribution to the dialogue on strategy. This analysis may provide inspiration and focus attention on thought-provoking patterns, rather than be viewed as a solution to follow strictly.

The strategic dialogue, a key theme in this book, and in strategic management control, is an appealing concept. Unfortunately, it is easier to name than to implement. The dialogues are graspable when conducted by two parties – for example, between partners, between manager and co-worker, or between co-workers. Typically, however, people at various levels participate in the strategic dialogues. The virtual organisation or network has chains of relationships. A company has hierarchical levels – and a number of functional groups. The challenge is to use the ideas presented in this book to identify which chains exist in the relevant organisation or which should exist. Not least important is to spot the missing chains and the broken chains. Additionally, it is important to settle on the ideal. Is it to achieve clear, common perceptions in all these chains – a maximally integrated control and complete strategic congruence? Is it to get first line managers and co-workers to be able to, and dare to, act independently by following their best understandings and instincts, with some horizontal and vertical contacts? Is it to insulate top management from the realities of actual operations to allow them to convincingly conduct a dialogue with investors, owners, community partners, analysts, politicians, and so on, undisturbed by rich insight into what is actually happening in operations (and without interfering with operations)? Or is a balance somewhere between these extremes preferable? We can offer no answers that are applicable to all situations; we can, however, encourage you to think about these questions and to discuss your ideas.

Another interesting question concerns how the organisation should manage the consequences of decisions. If there is responsibility, what are then the consequences of taking responsibility? Of not facing up to one's responsibility? And what are the consequences of taking responsibility, even though certain rules and formal control signals were not followed (or of choosing freely between contradicting signals)? The book has referred to the external requirements of, for example, the Sarbanes-Oxley Act on financial and internal control reporting. Such regulatory systems can result in the view that everything is sound as long as the formal requirements are met and the reporting is neat and tidy. The consequences of such requirements for those responsible are potentially only negative. The manager who presents a clean report has done what is expected, but cannot expect praise. Company leaders charged with corporate misrepresentations are sternly criticised. In worst-case scenarios, they resign, incur fines, or go to prison. Performance bonuses, on the other hand, may be awarded for good, or even acceptable, performance, according to rather narrowly defined indicators, but unacceptable performance rarely results in repayments or salary reductions.

What is the situation for the co-workers? Do they receive both praise and blame? Rewards and punishments? Or constructive criticism? And are such outcomes based on feedback evaluations that are specific or vague? In some organisations, feedback is one-sided: blame or punishment only – or praise or rewards only. In some organisations, there is no feedback, only silence. People must decide whether their actions and decisions led to good or blameworthy results.

How are rewards and punishments determined? Which perspective on human character prevails? Is it more of the principal-agent theory view that agents are selfish and require close supervision or forcible incentives in order to act in line with the principal's interests? Or is it, rather, the idea that everyone strives to perform well and act in the best interests of the organisation? Although the book does not develop these ideas extensively, the issue of consequences should be an essential and rigorously discussed aspect of the strategic management control dialogues. If not, strategic management control will be skewed.

In these concluding remarks, we think it is appropriate to summarise some of the book's messages and common themes. First, all the authors emphasise the importance of dialogue for strategic management control. Of course, planning and monitoring processes should be systematic and analytical. However, these processes should include the co-workers when the discussions turn to organisational direction, standards and goals. Management should also invite the co-workers' participation in the analysis of results. Only then do they really participate in the control, and are enabled to contribute to the strategy and the realisation of it. In this context, we agree with Robert Simons, who in his publications emphasises that it is the use of management controls, rather than their design, that contributes to results.

Second, after the importance of dialogue, several chapters note that the division between the formulation of strategy and its implementation is too simplistic. On-going management control and the formulation of strategy are linked. Metrics in planning and monitoring should be based in organisational strategy (rather than in external accounting standards or industry practice), and the results according to these strategy-based metrics should of course alert co-workers and managers to when and if the strategy needs reassessment. It is important in this connection to recognise that the design and use of management control is a kind of "filter" or a "pair of spectacles" that managers and co-workers use when they analyse the organisation and its external environment. Thus, strategic management control determines to a considerable extent what is deemed important at any particular moment. Thereby, it also has a major influence on the assessment of the organisation's strategy, and on how future strategies are formulated.

Third, the design of the organisation's control mix (and its control package) poses a difficult challenge. The control mix should provide clear signals on priorities. It should also remind managers and co-workers of the complexity of operations and of the need to balance seemingly contradictory goals in the short term and long term. The claim in this book is that the organisation's strategy should be the natural point of reference when goals are in focus. Contradictions in the control mix can be justified as long as they are clearly motivated and are explained in sufficient detail in communications on strategy.

At this point, our book concludes. We hope this discussion of the elements in strategic management control benefits students, researchers and practitioners. The book is our description of the complexity of strategic management control, including its challenges. As we wrote in Chapter 1, one of our goals was to introduce and problematise issues rather than to present simple solutions to complex problems. The perspectives and approaches presented in the book are at the forefront of current research. The authors are practice-interested researchers, well-positioned in their respective fields. Because the book is forward-looking, it points to interesting areas for continued research (e.g. methods and technologies related to strategic management control).

Throughout, the book's chapters are rooted in the Scandinavian management tradition. The work of Professor Nils-Göran Olve (who is repeatedly cited in the book) reflects this tradition. His many publications and his role as appreciated mentor, instructor and lecturer have increased our understanding (and that of many others, in Sweden and abroad) of the relationship between strategy and management control. His focus – and ours – is on the need for a deeper dialogue between managers and co-workers, both within and between organisations.

INDEX